GUIDANCE MINI-LESSONS

60 Brief Power-Packed Activities

For Classrooms, Small Groups, Individuals & School-Wide

By
Diane Senn, Ed.S.

© 2013, 2012 by YouthLight, Inc.
Chapin, SC 29036

Design and Layout by Amy Rule
Project Editing by Susan Bowman and Brian Leiby

ISBN: 978-1-59850-110-0

Library of Congress Number
2011940949

10 9 8 7 6 5 4 3 2 1
Printed in the United States

ACKNOWLEDGEMENTS

A sincere thank you to the following...

To the children whose excitement in learning, listening, doing, growing, building confidence... continues to amaze and encourage us as helping professionals to continue the support... thank you!

To Kathy McElvenny, fellow counselor and friend, who not only takes the time to listen and brainstorm with me but also gave of her time to review and edit each page... thank you!

To Amy Rule, graphic designer and friend, who makes the magic happen with her graphic skill and design...thank you!

To Bob and Susan Bowman, presidents of YouthLight, Inc., for their willingness in supporting and providing feedback and encouragement for this project... thank you!

To my husband Stan, for his encouragement, willingness, and support he gives to continue this adventure of writing... thank you!

And most importantly we give honor and thanks to God, our guiding light!

TABLE OF CONTENTS

TABLE OF CONTENTS

INTRODUCTION

This book provides 60 brief guidance activities (mini-lessons), which cover a wide range of topics across the three domains of personal/social, academic, and career development. These activities can be used in a variety of settings:

in **CLASS LESSONS** as an add-on to a lesson or used to build a lesson from the activity,

in **INDIVIDUAL COUNSELING** to provide a creative way to address needs, build skills, and to personalize for your student,

in **SMALL GROUP COUNSELING** as a fun way to prompt discussions and provide follow-up for skill building,

SCHOOL-WIDE through televised morning announcements or assembly program as a "spotlight" or "commercial" in the regular program. This is a great way to connect with all of your students at once – it's effective and efficient!

Using these power-packed activities will capture your students' attention, mix in some fun, and most important, provide opportunities for learning. You will find 7 sections in this book, each with activities using different approaches to engage your students. The sections are:

LEARNING THROUGH EVERYDAY OBJECTS – selects everyday objects and connects them to learning skills with the intent of the object serving as a tangible reminder of the skill learned.

CANDY LAND OF LESSONS – Candy is a great attention-getter and many common candies can make your lessons memorable! This section uses everyday candy to highlight different learning concepts. Using candy in your activities can also serve as an external reward/incentive for skill improvement. You may want to consider the following so we don't 'over do it' with candy:

- You can use the wrappers from the candy and not the actual candy. The wrapper may be enough to capture their attention and create the learning connection.

- You may choose to use the candy as an incentive/reward when the student has put the new skill into action. Caution is given here to give candy responsibly and if used as an external reward, process to connect to the internal reward of the good feeling of goal achievement.

- Use small portions of candy: a few M&M's or Skittles, mini or bite size candy bars, etc. rather than the whole pack or full size bar.

INTRODUCTION

POSTER POWER FOR LEARNING – Posters are great for visual learners! The poster activities take learning to the next level by providing a variety of discussions, role-plays, exercises, and self-reflection using the poster information. The posters, when displayed in the classrooms or hallways, continue the learning through the visual reinforcement.

LEARNING THROUGH REFLECTION WRITING – provides the structure to help your student process – to write as they think and to think as they write – and personalize different learning concepts. The skill of putting your thoughts in writing becomes a lifelong tool of insight and learning through writing.

BRIEF SKITS FOR LEARNING – Great for your kinesthetic learners! Students will learn not only through participating in the role play but also from seeing the desired skill in action.

KALEIDOSCOPE OF ACTIVITIES – a kaleidoscope or variety of fun activities for learning.

MARVELOUS MAGIC TRICKS FOR LEARNING – Students always seem to be intrigued with magic tricks so why not use that attraction to engage them in learning? This section will show you how to perform a few easy tricks and the lessons that can be related to the tricks.

A SIDE NOTE
Since I use magic tricks on a regular basis I ask the students to follow 3 rules:

> Rule #1: You can't ask me how I did it – I'm not going to tell.
>
> Rule #2: If you know the trick, don't tell.
>
> Rule #3: You have to learn something from the trick.

I emphasize #3 since that is the point of including the trick! Typically I am low-key with the word "magic" and simply emphasize the word "trick." When students are completing their last grade with me I usually show and teach them the "trick" called BAG POP TRICK – see Activity 52.

The 60 activities cover a wide range of topics. Review the **TABLE OF CONTENTS** for the topics listed in parentheses after each activity title. Or, look in the **INDEX** for a listing of topics correlated to the activities.

Most importantly this book is intended to **HELP YOU… HELP CHILDREN!**… Enjoy!

LEARNING THROUGH EVERYDAY OBJECTS

The activities in this section selects everyday objects and connects them to learning skills with the object serving as a tangible reminder of the skill learned.

CRAYON - PUT INTO ACTION

Purpose

To reinforce that our actions, what we choose to do, puts our 'mark' on life. Activity can be used as an introduction to a service learning project.

Materials

✓ Box of crayons

Procedure

Hold up a crayon and ask others what they see? The typical answer will be just a stick of crayon.

Next take the crayon and draw a picture with the color you have such as drawing the sun with the yellow crayon, or a tree with the green, etc. Share that when the crayon is put into action it can become something wonderful – a beautiful picture.

Now ask for a student to come up front and ask your student what they see. Emphasize how when we first look at a person we often see just a person – what we see on the outside but then...

Ask the person to smile... and say: **"When they smile they connect with others and can brighten someone's day."**

Ask the person to pretend they are helping the teacher hand out papers... and say: **"They are just a person but when they are put into action helping someone they can do wonderful things..."**

This introduction is great as a lead into a service learning project that may be planned. Share that each of us is just a person but that when we go into action helping others and working together we can create a beautiful picture of helping others. You may choose to take a picture of the helping project in action and relate back to your crayon picture.

Pose a question at the end: **"What will you do with your life in the future? What will your action be?"**

HONESTY REPUTATION

Purpose

To review the reputation of Abraham Lincoln as exemplifying the character trait of Honesty.

Materials

✓ Pennies

Procedure

I have typically shared this mini-lesson on our televised morning announcements – what a wonderful way to reach all students at once!

Introduce the word "reputation" and say: **"A reputation is how others see you and that you get a reputation by how you act over and over again."**

Hold up a penny and ask: **"Which president is on the penny?"** Usually some of the students in the TV studio are eager to answer the question but if no one is around, offer the answer of **"Abraham Lincoln."**

Then ask: **"Does anyone know Abraham Lincoln's nickname?"** Share that he has become known as "Honest Abe" because he always was honest in what he did and how he acted.

The fun came after announcements when I went in and out of as many classrooms as I could in 15 minutes - carrying a pocket full of pennies. I quizzed the students about what they heard on the morning show. I asked them such questions as, "What does reputation mean?" or "What president is on the penny?" or "What is Abraham Lincoln's nickname?" or "What does it mean to be honest?" As students answered correctly I gave the student a penny. It was amazing to see how excited they were to get the penny. On the way out the door I reinforced it with some thought questions: **"How do you act over and over again? What reputation do you have? Is it one of honesty?"**

Caution: Always ask your teacher first if you may enter and interrupt the class for a moment. And, as always, use your judgment as to if the interruption will be received well.

BEACH BALL BUZZ - CHARACTER*

Purpose

To provide an active, fun way to review or discuss different topics of character, study skills, anger management, and self-concept.

Materials

✓ Beach ball(s) (beach balls with the six sections work best) You will need a beach ball for each topic if you choose to create all 4 topics.

✓ Permanent marker

Preparation

With permanent marker, write one of the following questions/statements in each segment on the ball. Note that a silly direction is also added for the fun of the game. Questions/Statements:

SUGGESTED QUESTIONS FOR **CHARACTER**:
- Give an example of 'being respectful'.
- Why is 'being honest' important?
- Name a responsibility you have at school.
- What does 'having good character' mean?
- What does cooperation mean?
- Hop like a frog.

SUGGESTED QUESTIONS FOR **STUDY SKILLS**:
- What is your favorite subject and why?
- Where is your best place to study and do your homework?
- How do you handle distractions when you are trying to listen and concentrate?
- What is your advice to someone about how to do well in school?
- Share a good way to keep schoolwork organized.
- Clap your hands 3 times and hop like a bunny.

SUGGESTED QUESTIONS FOR **ANGER MANAGEMENT**:
- Show us how to take three deep breaths when you are angry.
- Name one thing that happens to your body when you are getting angry.
- Share a time when you got angry.
- Name one thing that helps you calm down when you are angry.
- Sing the "ABC" song out loud.
- Pretend you are a bird and fly around the room.

SUGGESTED QUESTIONS FOR **SELF-CONCEPT**:
- Name something that you can do well.
- Tell about something you have done recently that you feel proud about.
- I feel happy when...
- What do you tell yourself when you make a mistake?
- Name something that you have fun doing.
- Crow like a rooster.

Procedure

Have your students stand up and spread out in the room. Direct them to toss the ball to another student in the group. As that student catches the ball check to see where their right pointer finger is on the ball. The student must then answer that question or do what it says to do. Expand the discussion when appropriate.

If more control is needed with the ball toss have the student, before tossing the ball, call the name of the student they are throwing the ball to.

*adapted with permission from Beach Ball Fun Activity from Small Group Counseling for Children (Grades 2-5) by Senn, YouthLight, Inc.

ERASE AND TRY AGAIN

Purpose

To emphasize the importance of learning from our mistakes and trying again.

Materials

✓ Assortment of erasers and white out

Procedure

Ask your students to describe the purpose of erasers and white-out.

Review that erasers and white-out are used when we have made a mistake on paper and need to make changes.

Ask: **Do people make mistakes in life?** Ask for examples. Share examples of mistakes we make not only on paper but in life with learning new things, in getting along with others, and in our behavior choices.

Relate that the eraser for 'life's mistakes' is our **brain,** to learn from what we did wrong and to make the correction.

Add the comment: **We're lucky to be able to always carry our brain around with us!**

"I CAN FIX THIS!"

"I LEARNED NOT TO DO THAT AGAIN."

"I DIDN'T GET IT RIGHT THE FIRST TIME BUT I CAN TRY AGAIN."

© YouthLight, Inc.

MAGIC WAND – MAKE STRESS DISAPPEAR

Purpose

To review strategies for relieving stress.

Materials

✓ Pencil, pen, or marker covered with black construction paper or black contact paper with a white tip to resemble a magic wand (white out works great to create the white tip on the end of the black construction or contact paper).

✓ Paper and pencils

Procedure

With your magic wand (pencil, pen, or marker), write the word STRESS vertically on a paper or board.

Ask: **What is stress?** Ask the student(s) to share a time they may have felt stressed or worried. Share that stress is a part of our lives.

Explain that some stress is good for us because it keeps us focused and thinking, but too much stress or worry can weigh us down and not be healthy for us.

Share: **To help us deal with stress in a healthy way we can use our magic wand** (pencil, pen, or marker) **to help. Let's see what magical message it has to share.** Write the key words given below and share, discuss, ask questions, give examples, role-play, etc.

S: **Self-Awareness** of body cues

Explain that our body reacts to stress in different ways - by our tightening of our muscles, being tired, by our breathing, "butterflies in the stomach," etc. Explain the importance of tuning in to our body cues and being aware of stress so we can effectively deal with the stress. Have your student(s) draw an outline of their body and indicate areas their body responds to when they are stressed, for examples: their head for headache, stomach for "butterflies in the stomach," clenched fist for tight muscles, etc.)

T: Talk

Share that talking about what we are worried or stressed about can help us think through the problem. Ask students to name people in their lives they can talk with. Also include talking to yourself through journaling, or talking to your pet, or stuffed animal as a way to process the problem.

R: Rest

Explain the importance of getting the right amount of rest. Explain that our mind does not think well when we haven't gotten a good night's sleep. (Need to also include the caution of too much rest when used as an avoidance).

E: Exercise

Review how exercise can help energize the body and promote thinking. Practice different exercises.

S: Stop Worrying

Share that when a person has a problem and he/she is not thinking about a solution or way to manage the problem then it is called "worrying." Explain that worrying does not change the situation but focusing on being a problem solver does. Any thinking beyond that is worrying and worrying is a waste of time and energy.

S: Smile It Away!

Explain the benefit of a positive attitude in any situation.

Review the key words in STRESS for helping to manage stress.

Allow the student to turn their own pencil into a magic wand by covering it with the black construction or contact paper and white tip. Remind the student to "make stress disappear" by writing out and applying the key words in STRESS management.

16

FLOWERS: LATE BLOOMERS

Materials

✓ Full bloom flower and a flower bud
   (artificial flowers work fine)

Procedure

Ask students to share what stories they have heard about learning to walk. The typical story involves taking a wobbly step or two and falling and then trying again and again until success. Include in the discussion how babies seem to continue trying over and over again to walk that they don't get defeated and give up...

Ask the students if they have any trouble walking now.

Point out how babies learn to walk at different ages: some as early as 1 year and some as late as 2 ½ years.

Next compare the flower in full bloom with the flower bud. Discuss how the bud, in its time, will also be a beautiful flower in full bloom. You can take the discussion further asking: **Just because the flower bud isn't blooming as quickly as the other flower do you stop watering it and taking care of it?**

Finally make the connection to different learning experiences that your student may be experiencing – perhaps first learning to read, perhaps learning multiplication facts, etc.

Ask the questions: **Is it okay for flowers to bloom at different times? Is it okay for people to learn things at different times? Should we ever give up if learning is hard or other people around us seemed to have already learned it? Do you think that skill we are trying to learn will be easy for us one day?**

Purpose

To point out that every student learns at different rates and at different times but once it has been learned it's learned.

17

BEACH SHELLS - ONE IN A MILLION

© Youthlight Inc

Purpose

To appreciate the uniqueness of each person.

Materials

✓ Container of similar but different seashells (can use fall leaves or the idea of snowflakes to communicate the same lesson – choose what your students will relate best to)

Procedure

Ask: **What do you know about seashells? Have you ever or seen anyone ever walk along the beach shore collecting shells? Why do people pick up shells?**

Continue the discussion of how each shell is different, unique, or one of a kind and yet each one is beautiful in different ways.

Have each student select a shell, study it, appreciate the uniqueness of the shell, and then put in back with the group of other shells. Next have the student locate their shell and share with the group what was unique about their shell and what they appreciate about the shell.

Ask students: **How is a beach shell and a person the same?** Broaden the discussion to include how each person is unique, special, appreciated, part of something larger, and it's important to take time to study (get to know) and appreciate each person…

THE COMBINATION TO UNLOCKING YOUR SUCCESS*

Purpose

To provide a guideline to create an individual success plan for academic, personal, social, or emotional growth. This activity is written to be used with an individual however with some variations it can be adapted for a small group or class.

Materials

- ✓ Lockable box decorated as a treasure box
- ✓ Combination lock
- ✓ Appropriate reward for reaching goal (treat, certificate, congratulations note, etc.)
- ✓ Copy of the worksheet on page 20.

Preparation

Place the selected reward for achieving the goal in the "treasure box" and lock with the combination lock.

Procedure

Discuss a particular goal the student may be working on whether it is to work on making friends, to managing anger, or an academic goal in reading or math.

Next, ask the student to open the locked treasure box. Student's typical response is "I can't – it's locked – I don't know the combination."

Ask the student if he/she has ever opened a combination lock before? Point out that each lock, even though they may look the same on the outside, has a different set or combination of numbers that are needed to unlock the lock. Relate that we are like that combination lock that each student must find the right combination or strategies to reach their goal and to unlock his/her success.

Brainstorm together to create a personalized plan of strategies for the student to achieve their selected goal. Use the worksheet on page 20 to outline and document the plan.

To continue the analogy of the combination lock and the combination to the individual's success, give the student one number in the combination lock each time progress is being made in their plan. Once all the numbers for the combination lock have been shared and the student has progressed to his/her goal, allow the student to unlock the treasure box to find a reward, treat, or certificate in the box for their hard work. Don't forget to emphasize that the "real" reward is in the success of achieving the goal.

*adapted from Senn's "Combination to Academic Success" from
Creative Approaches for Counseling Individual Children. Youthlight, Inc. 1-800-209-9774

_____'S PLAN TO UNLOCKING SUCCESS

GOAL: Specific area I want to improve is _____

_____

_____ .

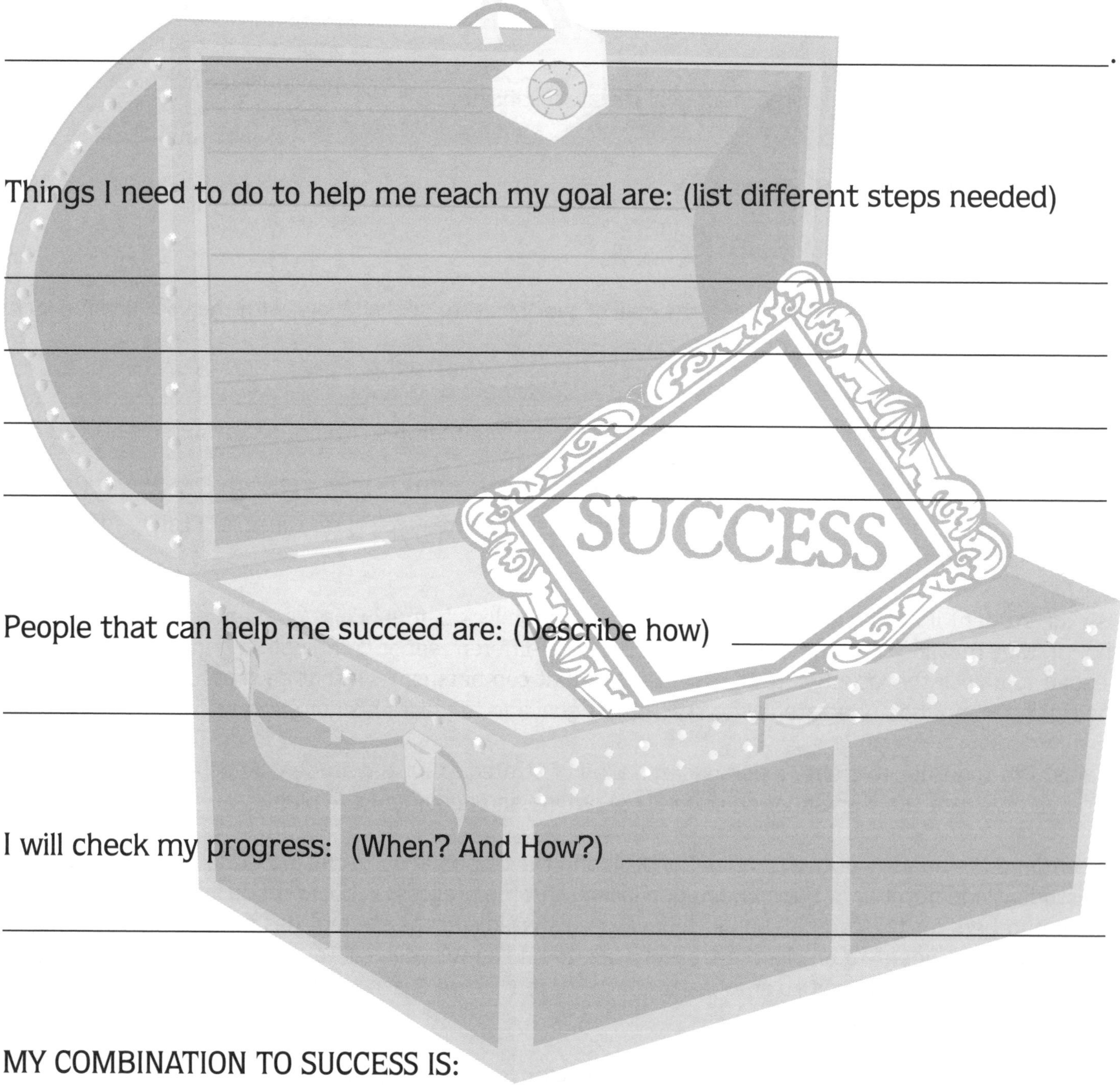

Things I need to do to help me reach my goal are: (list different steps needed)

_____

_____

_____

_____

SUCCESS

People that can help me succeed are: (Describe how) _____

_____

I will check my progress: (When? And How?) _____

_____

MY COMBINATION TO SUCCESS IS:

_____   _____

BLOCK THE BURN OF TEASING

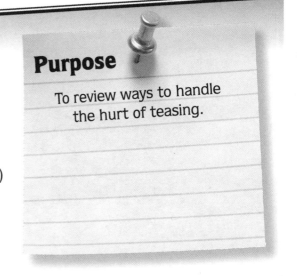

Purpose

To review ways to handle the hurt of teasing.

Materials

✓ Sunblock

✓ Picture of the sun with the words "Friends/Others" (pg. 22)

✓ Picture of the sunblock bottle outline (pg. 22)

✓ Markers

Procedure

Ask: **When you are out in the sun all day, maybe at field day or the beach or out playing, what does your parent remind you to put on to keep from getting a sun burn?** (sunblock)

Ask: **Is the sun good or bad?** (Point out that it can be both. It is good in that we need it for things to grow and for us to be healthy and it helps in providing the light of the day. It can be bad that too much sun is harmful to our skin. Share that we value the sun so we take the bad with the good)

Ask: **Should we always hide from the sun since it is bad for our skin or should we find a way to protect our skin from the harm of the sun so we can enjoy being out and about?**

Point out that sunblock is available to help protect our skin from the harm of the sun so we can still enjoy being outside. Discuss how sunblock works: it takes time to apply but is worth it, it provides a barrier to prevent harmful rays from getting into the skin, you have to reapply the sunblock after a time period or after swimming…

Display the picture of the sun and relate how we can think of the sun as "friends/others." Ask student(s) to share the 'good' and 'bad' of friends.

Ask: **How can we protect ourselves from the teasing and the harm of friends – what will be our 'sunblock' to protect us?**

On the large bottle of sunblock write the different strategies that protect us from the harm of our friends when they are teasing, making fun of us, or leaving us out.

BLOCK THE BURN OF TEASING

BE YOUR OWN REFEREE - PLAY FAIR

Material

✓ Whistle

Purpose

To emphasize the importance of fairness.

Procedure

Ask: **Have you ever watched a sports game in person, on TV, or played on a sports team before? During an official game, who makes sure that the rules are followed and the game is being played fair?** (referee) **What does the referee use to get others' attention, to pause the game, when a rule has been broken?** (whistle).

Blow the whistle for effect…

Ask: **We've talked about sports games but how about in life. Are there times in life when we are tempted not to be fair with someone else? Do we need to blow our whistle on ourselves, to pause, and think about what we just said or did?**

Say: **Our "Golden Rule" is: Treat others how we want to be treated. How does this apply to being fair? Would we like it if someone else doesn't share, or take turns, or if they try to cheat or blame us for their mistake.**

For each statement below ask the student to answer FAIR or UNFAIR and then GUILTY or NOT GUILTY to indicate if they have done that before.

1. Break in line.
2. Sharing with your brother or sister.
3. Say that it is someone's fault when it's not.
4. Lying to get out of something.
5. Cheating to win the game.
6. Not letting others have a turn on the swings, playing video games, etc.
7. Willing to play or do things your friend would like to do.
8. Saying you have to study so you don't have to do chores.

Discuss a plan for improvement or a reminder to continue being fair. Copy, cut out the picture of the whistle, write the plan on the whistle, and encourage the student to take and display as a reminder.

GUIDED BY YOUR INTERNAL COMPASS

Purpose

To make good choices that point our lives in the right direction.

Materials

✓ Compass

✓ Copy of the Internal Compass on page 25.

Procedure

Together look at a compass and discuss the purpose of a compass. Include in the discussion that a compass helps us find the right direction.

Share: **Life is full of choices that determine the direction of our life. Consider the following 3 questions to be our compass in life to help us make good choices:**
   1. **Does it break a rule or law?**
   2. **Will anyone be hurt? Physically or emotionally?**
   3. **Would my teacher or parent be upset with my decision?**

Review the situations below. Apply the Internal Compass questions to determine if the choice heads you in the right direction.

   Your good friend suggested that you not let Susan join your friendship group at recess anymore. What should you do?

   You want to play your favorite video game rather than study for the big Social Studies test. What should you do?

   You really like the new key chain a student in your class bought at the school store this morning. The student put it just inside their desk and they are away at the water fountain. You are tempted to take the key chain. What should you do?

   While completing some class work, the teacher had to step outside the door to talk to an adult. She asked us not to talk and to continue with our class work. Everyone in the class is talking and John, a classmate, just asked you a question. What should you do?

   Your parent asked you to collect the trash and take it out but your friend is at the door asking you to come out and play. What should you do?

Summarize the use of the Internal Compass questions and remind student(s) that if any answers to the compass questions are YES then they need to reconsider their choice.

INTERNAL COMPASS

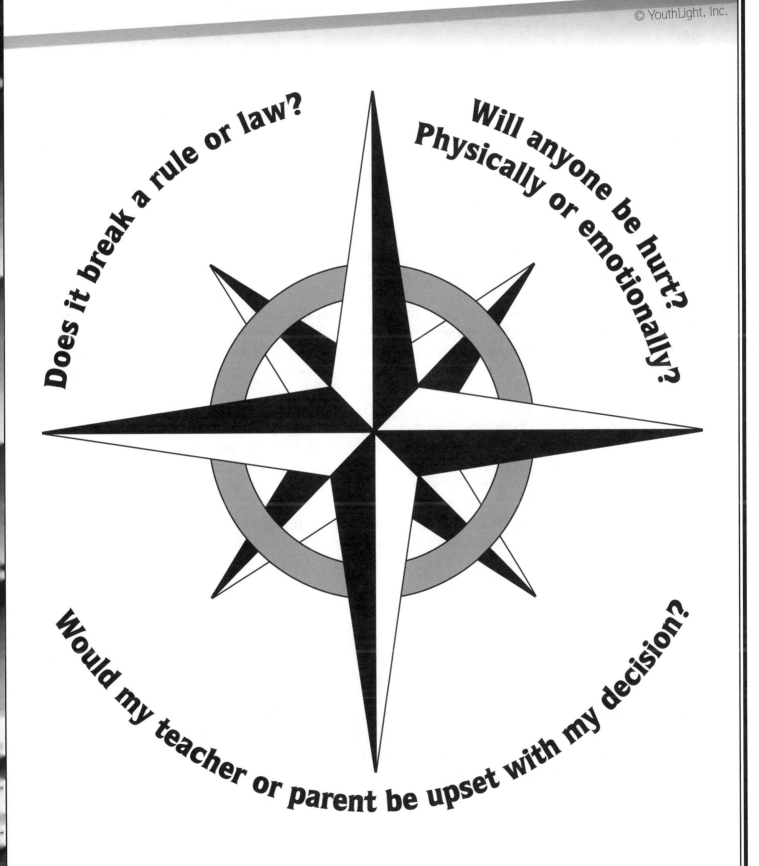

Does it break a rule or law?

Will anyone be hurt?
Physically or emotionally?

Would my teacher or parent be upset with my decision?

PREDICTIVE POWERS FOR PROBLEM SOLVING

Materials

- ✓ Clear balloon
- ✓ Small bowl

Procedure

Ask: **Do you agree that everything we say or do has an outcome or consequences?** Discuss and give examples.

Share: **When we have a problem, what we say or do about it – our actions – can either help the problem or make it worse. So how do we know what to do? Wouldn't it be nice if a crystal ball could really "see" into the future. We don't have a crystal ball that would work but we do have the next best thing - the ability to PREDICT or make an educated guess about what might happen if we said or did something.**

DEMONSTRATION ACTIVITY: To help students understand the concept of prediction, hold a balloon up and ask the students to predict or think about what will happen if you blow air into the balloon. Typical answer is to inflate or get larger. Proceed to test out the prediction by blowing air into the balloon and holding the neck of the balloon with your fingers. With surprise, ask the student: **How did you know it was going to inflate or get larger?** Typical answer is because I've done it before. Reinforce the student's answer by explaining that the student had made a "prediction" or guess about what might happen based on previous experience. For fun, if you would like to try another prediction exercise, ask the students what would happen if you let go of the inflated balloon. Test out the prediction.

Make the connection that our 'powers of prediction' are like being able to see into the future. Explain that when we have a problem we need to consider or predict what might happen if we said or did a particular thing and then determine if that would be helpful or not. Remind students that predictions are based on our knowledge and past experiences. Emphasize that by taking the time to review and predict there is a better chance that we can have a better outcome in solving our problem.

Create a "pretend" crystal ball by inflating the balloon again but this time tie a knot in the balloon. Place the balloon in the small bowl and encourage students to pretend that it is a crystal ball that we can look into for our special powers to guess or predict the future or the outcome of our actions. Give examples of problems and possible choices in how to handle. Have students pretend to look into the crystal ball to "see into the future" and discuss what might be the outcome.

DON'T BE A BANANA BRUISER

Material

✓ Banana

Purpose

To understand the hurt and damage of indirect or social bullying.

Procedure

Say: **Name some physical kinds of bullying.** Include examples such as hitting, kicking, punching, etc. **What kind of marks may be left behind with the physical bullying?** Include examples such as bruises, cuts, bloody nose, etc.

Say: **Name some examples of indirect or social bullying.** Include examples such as teasing, exclusion, gossip, rumors, controlling, manipulation, etc. **What marks are left behind with the indirect or social bullying?**

BANANA DEMONSTRATION*: To help the student understand the hurt of indirect or social bullying, display a banana and ask the student(s) to think of this banana as a person for a moment. Review the examples of indirect/social bullying and as you share each example press your thumb into the banana on the outside of the peel. After several examples have been shared, examine the banana to see if there are any marks on the outside of the peeling. No marks are noticeable at this time but peel the banana, examine, and you will find bruise marks on the inside left by the thumb imprints. Make the connection relating that indirect/social bullying doesn't leave marks on the outside of the body such as the physical bullying, but indirect/social bullying leaves bruises on the inside. Point out that this hurt can often do more damage than physical bullying.

*source unknown

CANDY LAND OF LESSONS

This section uses everyday candy to highlight different learning concepts. The idea of candy seems to capture students' attention – even teachers!

M&M® BELIEF*

Purpose

To reinforce that the important part of people is on the inside, who they are, not how they look on the outside.

Format

Concept explained here can be introduced on the televised morning announcements with class teacher follow-up, or shared as part of a class or small group lesson.

Materials

✓ M&M's® for each student enough so the teacher can give each student a couple of M&M's® to run the "experiment."

✓ Teacher direction note copied for each class, attached to the M&M's® and given to teachers.

Procedure

Review with the students the different colors on the outsides of the M&M's®. Ask whether people eat the M&M's® because of the outside coating or the inside chocolate. Reinforce to the student that the outside color doesn't matter, it's the inside chocolate that is good.

For fun run the M&M® experiment: Blindfold a student volunteer, place an M&M® in his/her hand for them to eat and ask them to guess the color. Process how the color is just a guess but confirm with them that the good part is on the inside.

Relate the concept of outside vs. inside of the M&M® to the outside and inside of other people in that it doesn't matter what people look like on the outside – their size, shape, color, etc. but that it is who they are on the inside that is the good part and most important.

Let students know that they will be able to conduct their own experiment in their class with the M&M's®. Remind students that as they enjoy the good chocolate on the inside let it remind them about taking the time to get to know people for it is who people are on the inside that is the good part.

See the Teacher Memo and the M&M® Belief Poster on pages 31-32 for teacher follow-up activity. Copy the memo and poster, attach with a bag of M&M's®, and distribute to teachers.

*Activity adaptations from Sitsch and Senn's Puzzle Pieces, Youthlight, Inc.

TEACHER MEMO

To: Classroom Teachers

From: Your School Counselor

Re: M&M® Belief class follow-up activity

SUMMARY

On _____ morning we plan to share a mini-lesson on RESPECT on the televised morning announcements. We are emphasizing the importance of showing respect by not judging others on the outside (size, shape, color) but getting to know the person on the inside (the good things about them). We will do an M&M® experiment on the show in which we can't tell the color of the M&M® by the taste – so the color of the M&M® doesn't matter - and that the best part of the M&M® is the chocolate on the inside. Thus relating it to… it doesn't matter the color of a person's skin, eyes, or hair, their size, or their shape but what is important is what is INSIDE (the kind of person they are). We need to treat ourselves and others with RESPECT – looking for the best.

ACTIVITY

Share a few M&M's® with each student for them to conduct their own taste test (doesn't matter the color on the outside, the good part is the chocolate on the inside.) Remind students as they eat their M&M®, that the important part of people is on the inside – look for the good in others. Attached is an M&M® Belief Poster for your class to color and post in your classroom as a visual reminder.

M&M® BELIEF...

AS WITH THE M&M'S...

IT DOESN'T MATTER THE COLOR OF A PERSON'S SKIN, EYES OR HAIR, THEIR SIZE, OR THEIR SHAPE...

WHAT IS IMPORTANT IS WHAT IS INSIDE.

TREAT OURSELVES AND OTHERS WITH RESPECT!

CHILL WITH PEPPERMINT PATTY

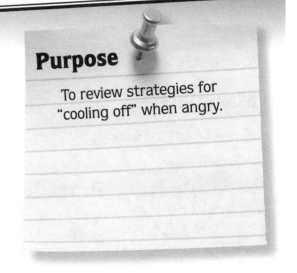

Purpose

To review strategies for "cooling off" when angry.

Materials

✓ Peppermint patties

Procedure

Ask the student to eat half of a peppermint patty and describe the taste. Ask if they have seen the commercials advertising peppermint patties with the theme of "…cool, refreshing taste that takes you away…get the sensation." Discuss the meaning.

Ask: **Have you ever had situations in life that you needed to cool down from or perhaps "be taken away" or to leave?** Talk about how when we are angry we need to calm down and cool off so we can think. Discuss how difficult it is to calm down when we keep thinking about how mad we are, how unfair, etc. It can help us calm down when we can move away from or leave the situation but sometimes we can't always leave so an important strategy to help us with our anger management is to take a mental break. Even if we can't always physically leave the situation we can leave the situation in our mind and instead think about something cooling and pleasant. This can help us calm down and cool off so we can think better. Relate this type of thinking to the message of the peppermint patty, "…cool, refreshing taste that takes you away…"

Ask the student to share several cooling thoughts – that "takes them away."

Have the student draw pictures of their cooling thoughts. Allow the student to eat the rest of their peppermint patty as they think and draw their pictures.

Offer to tape the wrapper of the peppermint patty on the page by their picture as a visual reminder of the lesson.

BE A "SMARTIE" WITH GOOD BEHAVIOR

Materials

✓ Smarties® Candy

Be respectful.

People are more important than things.

I'm not always going to get my way.

Cooperate.

Listen.

Maybe I will get to do it another day.

Work before play.

Be responsible.

Purpose

To reinforce good behavior choices.

Procedures

Ask the student to read the label on the candy.

Ask: **What does it mean to 'be smart'?** Include in the discussion that being smart doesn't only mean making A's in math, reading, etc. but that being smart also means making good choices in what we will do and how we will act. Ask: **Have you ever made a choice in how to act (what you said or did) and it got you in more trouble?**

If you are working with an individual student, tailor the discussion to that student's specific needs.

Open the pack of Smarties® Candy and together brainstorm smart thoughts that would help make good choices about behavior. For each thought that the student agrees would be helpful, have them write it down or write it down for them. The student can eat the candy circle for each good thought created. Challenge them to create as many good thoughts as there are candy circles in the package – remind them that different thoughts may be helpful for different situations.

If you are using this activity with a class, have the students divide into smaller groups and work together to create a list of good thoughts as guidelines in making good choices. Allow groups to share their list with the whole class.

YOU'RE A STARBURST

Materials

✓ Starburst® candy

✓ Copy of "You're the Starburst" Worksheet on page 36 for each student.

Procedure

Allow the student(s) to enjoy a piece of Starburst® candy. Ask the student(s) to describe the taste. Point out that as the candy is being enjoyed the good flavor comes out – bursting with flavor.

Ask: **What do you think it means if we compare the Starburst® candy to a person and say that each person is bursting with flavor?** Relate the word "flavor" to what is valuable, important, unique about a person.

Ask the student(s) to share the "flavor in them," in other words what is important, unique, and valuable – their capabilities and good qualities.

Ask the student(s) to write their good qualities and capabilities on the body outline of the "You're the Starburst" Worksheet. They may choose to put 'good listener' by the ears of the body outline, 'caring' by the heart, 'helping others' by the hands, etc.

As you review the points they wrote on their body outline, tape a Starburst® candy by each. Allow the student(s) to take their starburst body outline with them, to refer to and remind them of their importance and value, and as they choose to eat the starburst candy from their body outline to remind themselves of the wonderful flavor in who they are.

Purpose

To focus on the importance and value of the individual.

© YouthLight Inc.

35

YOU'RE THE STARBURST

THE LIFESAVER PLAN

Purpose

To review helpful strategies when anxious, stressed or overwhelmed.

Materials

✓ Lifesavers® candy

✓ Copy of "Your Lifesaving Plan" Worksheet on page 38 for each student.

Procedure

Display the candy lifesavers. Ask what comes to mind when they hear the name of the candy. Discuss the purpose of a life saver on a ship or around a pool, swimming area, etc. Summarize that a lifesaver is used when someone is having trouble in the water – a lifesaver is a device that can pull them to safety.

Share the following fun fact about the naming of the candy lifesaver: In 1912 Clarence Crane realized that his chocolate candy didn't do well in the summer heat so he created a summer candy – a peppermint candy. At this same time, ships were beginning to use round life preservers so Crane created little round mints with holes in them and called them "Crane's Peppermint Life Savers." In 1924 he started making fruit flavored solid circles, in 1929 he added the holes to the fruit flavored circles, and in 1935 he put together the five flavor roll of Life Savers that we see today in stores.*

Summarize that the candy lifesaver was actually named after a device to help when you are in trouble.

Ask the student(s) to share a time when they felt they had a problem with being stressed, worried, or overwhelmed.

Brainstorm together helpful strategies.

Enjoy the lifesavers as you continue to discuss.

Have the student create their "lifesaving plan" for when they are worried, stressed, or overwhelmed.

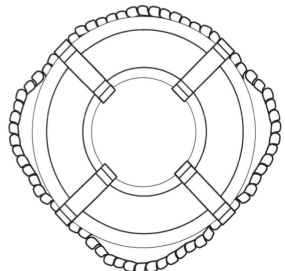

* information adapted from the following website: www.chevoncars.com/learn/food-recipes/candy-names

YOUR LIFESAVING PLAN

PROBLEM: _____

_____

PLAN: _____

_____

_____

HANDLING THE SOUR PATCH

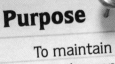

Purpose

To maintain a positive attitude even in difficult situations.

Materials

✓ Sour Patch Kids® candy

Procedure

Ask the student: **When you first think of candy does the word sweet or sour come to mind?** Emphasize that most candies are sweet however some candies are sour such as the sour patch candy. Ask if some people like the taste of the sour patch candy – explain how the sour patch candy is not completely sour but that some sugar has been added.

Eat and describe the taste of the sour patch candy.

Discuss the following saying that relates life experiences to candy: Life is sweet! But sometimes sour, so when it is - add some sugar or a positive thought.

Ask the student to give examples of when, "life is sweet!" Give examples of when, "life is sour."

Create specific "positive thoughts" that can help make the "sour" times "sweeter."

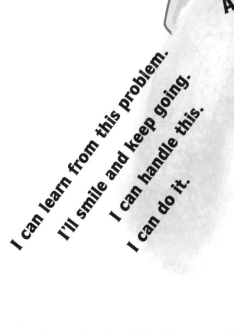

Adding the Sugar to the Sour Times

I can learn from this problem.

I'll smile and keep going.

I can handle this.

I can do it.

THE DUD IN MILK DUDS

Materials

✓ Milk Duds® candy

Purpose

To accept that no one is perfect but still important and valued.

Procedure

Look at the Milk Duds and ask if they have ever paid attention to the shape of each Milk Dud.

Share the following trivia about Milk Duds: In 1928 when the first Milk Duds were made the idea was to make them perfectly round. No matter how hard they tried they couldn't make them round so they decided to call them duds. The milk part comes from the large amount of milk used to make the candy. Even though they weren't perfect as first intended, the Milk Dud candy became a success.*

Discuss the following: **Are there times in life that we are not perfect? Are we still important and valued?** Relate examples the student gives about not being perfect to the success of the Milk Dud even though the perfect circle was not achieved. Point out the good aspects of the Milk Dud – the taste, texture, size… just as the student can point out good things about who they are.

Examine several Milk Duds to determine that each Milk Dud has its own unique shape.

Discuss the following sayings:

Life's Not Perfect.

Being Unique is Perfect!

Beauty is in the Eye of the Beholder.

Mistakes are Okay If We Learn From Them.

*information adapted from the following website: www.chevoncars.com/learn/food-recipes/candy-names

TAKE A FAST BREAK

Purpose

To provide an opportunity for students to create their own slogan from "Fast Break" that can help in life.

Materials

✓ Reese's Fast Break® candy bars

✓ Small poster board/chart paper and markers

Procedure

Discuss how commercials and ads are developed to promote their products. The intent is that their message and name of the product will "stick" with the person so they will buy the product. Let's see what you may remember. Ask students to complete the following: (Add additional slogans)

- "Give me a break, give me a break, break me off a piece of that _____." (Kit Kat Bar)

- "Eat more _____." (Chickin)

- "Like a good neighbor, _____ is there. (State Farm)

Display the candy bar and read the name "Fast Break." Brainstorm together something that would be helpful to learn or remember to help them in life that is connected with the words "Fast Break." Include such possibilities as: take a fast break to stop and think before saying or doing something; or take a fast break when you are angry to calm down; or take a fast break when you are being impulsive; etc.

Work in small groups or pairs and have each group create a slogan using the words "Fast Break" that can help them in life. Distribute poster board/chart paper and markers for students to write and decorate their slogan.

Let each group/pair present their slogan to the large group and discuss.

Allow students to eat a part of or a small Fast Break candy bar as they review their favorite slogan to help in life.

MOUNDS OF EXCITEMENT
TEACHER ACTIVITY

Materials

✓ Copies of the poem below for teachers with a small candy mounds bar attached.

Procedure

Place in teachers' boxes before they arrive on the first day of students. The note provides an extra treat and sets a positive tone to begin the year.

Purpose

To provide a fun note to teachers on the first day of school that students arrive.

Mounds of Excitement on the First Day of School!

Mounds of students cluttering the halls with books in hand.
Some with beaming faces,
Some tentative with a hint of shyness
And some faces still asleep…
Mounds of faces ready to learn.

Mounds of teachers/staff/administrators
Ready to inspire, support, and guide each child.
Mounds of faces ready to teach.

Mounds of learning, mounds of laughter,
Mounds of tears, mounds of joy,
Mounds of excitement
Once again resound through the halls of _____.
(School's name)

Welcome to a wonderful school year!
(Add your name)

YOU ARE 'MINT' TO HAVE A GREAT YEAR! TEACHER ACTIVITY

Purpose

To provide a supportive note to teachers for the first day of school.

Materials

✓ Copies of the saying below with a candy mint attached.

Procedure

Place in the teachers' boxes at the beginning of the year. The note provides an extra treat and sets a positive tone to begin the year.

> ### You are mint to have a great year!!
>
> ### Thank you for all that you do to make a difference in the lives of children.
>
> ### Let me know how I can be of help. . .
>
> ### YOUR SCHOOL COUNSELOR,

POSTER POWER FOR LEARNING

The poster activities take learning to the next level by providing a variety of discussions, role-plays, exercises, and self-reflection using the poster information.

WHAT DOES 'RESPECT' LOOK LIKE?

Purpose

To discuss and review examples of being respectful.

Materials

✓ 2 Copies of the "What Does Respect Look Like?" poster on page 47. One copy for display and the other cut into strips with single examples on each piece of paper.

Procedure

Define the word 'respect' and discuss why respect is important.

Review the information and pictures on the poster of what respect would "look like."

Divide being respectful into 4 categories and discuss each category:

Self-Respect

Respect for Others

Respect for Authority

Respect for Property

Ask students to categorize the examples on the poster as respect for self, others, authority or property.

Next, distribute the poster strips with single examples to students or pairs/groups of students. Ask the students to role play a specific example indicated by their paper or to give specific examples of what you may think, say, or do. To add a game feel to this activity, encourage the other students to guess what example they are sharing.

If time allows, have students create their own poster of examples of respect.

Challenge students to put their examples of respect into practice each and every day.

WHAT DOES RESPECT LOOK LIKE?

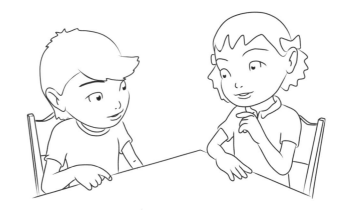

Appreciating the good things about yourself.

Saying nice things to others.

Appreciating each person's differences and uniqueness.

Listening when the person in charge asked you to do something.

Not interrupting others.

Using good manners in the classroom, in the cafeteria, on the bus... at our school.

Taking good care of things in our classroom, on our playground... at our school.

WHAT DOES 'BEING RESPONSIBLE' LOOK LIKE?

Purpose

To discuss and review examples of Being Responsible.

Materials

✓ Copy of the "What Does Being Responsible Look Like?" poster on page 49 for display and for each student.

✓ Optional: large pair of plastic silly glasses

Procedure

Define Responsible. Explain that being responsible touches every area of our life.

Explain that a word to describe Responsibility is "job." Share that we have jobs or responsibilities at home, at school, and in taking care of ourselves and we need to have responsible behavior in our choices we make in getting along with others.

Say: **To be responsible means to do what we are suppose to do, in other words to do our job. Let's look at what our Job Description at home would be.** (If you are choosing to use the silly glasses, put on the silly glasses yourself or on a volunteer as you say: 'let's see what being responsible LOOKS LIKE…" On the poster, review the responsibilities at home encouraging students to give examples of how to be responsible in each area. Add home responsibilities to the list.

Next, review the responsibilities at school that are listed on the poster. Discuss WHY each of the responsibilities is important. Add additional responsibilities to the list.

Finally, introduce the last section on the poster – being responsible with your behavior. Divide your group into smaller groups or pairs and ask the groups to choose responsibly following a class or school rule to role play. As the groups role-play, ask others to 'guess' what rule they are role-playing – discuss.

Continue discussing the poster including responsible ways to solve problems. Emphasize the importance to think before you act in order to be responsible for your words and actions.

Include a discussion of responsible choices to stay healthy.

Distribute copies of the poster for each student to color and display for reinforcement.

WHAT DOES BEING RESPONSIBLE LOOK LIKE?

RESPONSIBLE

AT HOME:

Do your job or chores

Help mom and dad

Get along with your brother or sister

Do your homework

AT SCHOOL:

On the bus…sit quietly and still

On the playground…play on the equipment in the right way

In the classroom… enter quietly, unpack, and begin your morning work

In the classroom… listen, participate, and complete your class work

WITH YOUR BEHAVIOR:

Follow class and school rules

Be a good problem solver: get the facts, handle your anger, and find a good way to solve the problem – share, take turns, talk it out, ignore, compromise…

Make healthy choices for your body: exercise, eat nutritious food, get your rest

A FRIEND IS...

Materials

✓ Copy of the "A Friend Is..." poster on page 51.

✓ Copy of the chart below

✓ Paper, pencil/markers

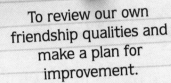

Purpose

To review our own friendship qualities and make a plan for improvement.

Procedure

Ask: **What is meant by the saying, to have a friend you must first be a friend?**

Direct students to review the A Friend Is... poster and describe how that trait can help in a friendship?

The chart below lists different friendship qualities ranging from those qualities that are helpful in a friendship to those qualities that are not helpful. Ask: **Where are you on the chart below? Put an X on the line that marks where you are with that friendship quality.**

Bossy ━━━━━━━━━━━	Cooperative
Whines ━━━━━━━━━━	Pleasant
Bullies ━━━━━━━━━━	Caring
Complains ━━━━━━━	Good Attitude
Name Caller ━━━━━	Shares Compliments
Talker ━━━━━━━━━━	Listener

Instruct the student to draw a picture of themselves and add their own friendship qualities they have and the friendship qualities they want to work on.

Encourage the student to post their picture as a visual reminder.

A FRIEND IS...

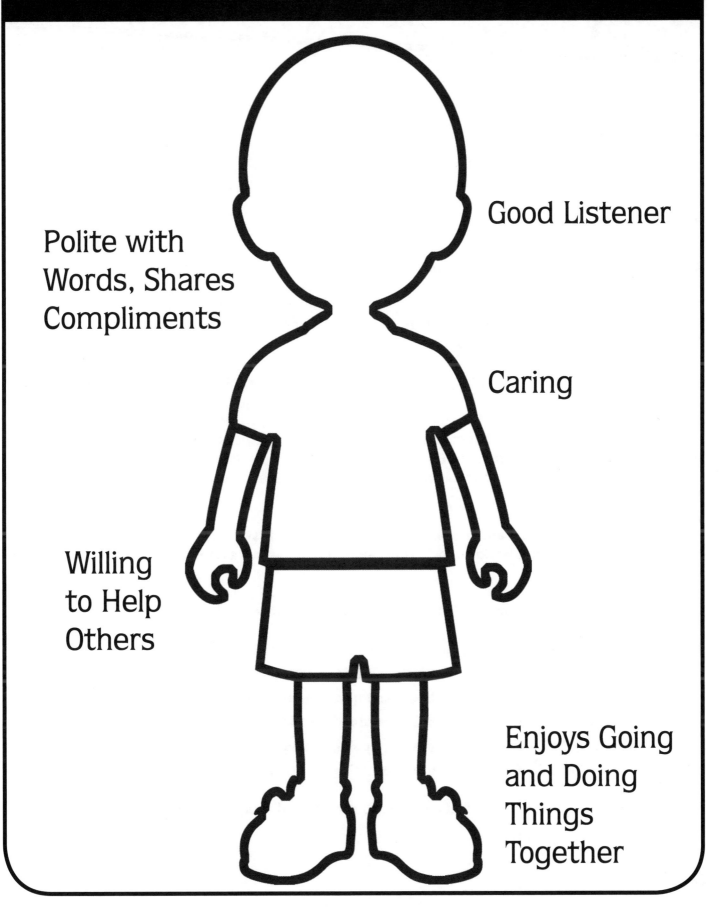

Good Listener

Polite with Words, Shares Compliments

Caring

Willing to Help Others

Enjoys Going and Doing Things Together

HOMEWORK HAPPINESS

Purpose

To provide study tips in structure and organization to help with homework.

Material

✓ Copy of the "Homework Happiness" poster on page 53.

Procedure

Ask: **What can happen if you just leave your time for homework to chance and don't schedule or set aside a specific time?**
Review that other things may get in the way – playing, TV, etc. and the day may be over before you realize you didn't do your homework.
Describe what you have found that is helpful for you scheduling homework time (a calendar with times? A chart? Same time each day?).

Ask: **Why do you think it would help to study in the same place each day?** Point out that our body develops habits that it responds to. For example, explain that you may not be thinking about art but when your class goes to the art room for class your body is ready or when you walk in the music room or PE room your body clicks in that direction. So if we train our body that when we sit in a specific place for homework that it is quiet time, focused time, ready to think - our body will change into that gear. Caution that our homework spot should not be in front of a TV, not on your bed, etc. Prefer at a desk or table.

Ask: **What would be the benefit to doing our hardest subject first?** Explain that you typically have more energy when you first sit down to do your homework and can tackle the hard subject better at first.

Ask: **What do you think is meant by 'Take Short Breaks Between Subjects'?**

Answer TRUE or FALSE for the following and explain your answer.
    TRUE or FALSE: Take a short break and watch a TV show.
    TRUE or FALSE: Take a short break and go to the refrigerator and fix a snack.
    TRUE or FALSE: Take a short break by standing and stretching.
    TRUE or FALSE: Take a short break by going outside and playing.
    TRUE or FALSE: Take a short break by doing 5 jumping jacks.

Say: **Show me one quick exercise you could do to stretch and energize the body so you can focus back on work.**

HOMEWORK HAPPINESS

STUDY TIPS FOR HOMEWORK...

Do It and Get It Done!

Schedule a Set Study Time Each Day.

Do Your Hardest Subjects First.

MATH

SCIENCE

Take Short Breaks Between Subjects.

Study in the Same Place Each Day.

GROWING FROM MISTAKES

Materials

✓ 2 copies of the "Growing From Mistakes" poster on page 55. One for display and one to cut out the message flowers for discussion.

Purpose

To review how we can learn from our mistakes and grow to be a better person.

Procedure

Ask: **What do you think the word "grow" means on the poster "Growing from Mistakes?"** Relate that "grow" means "to learn from – to help us be a better person.

Review the important message of each flower on the poster. Have students select a flower and explain or lead a discussion about the message of the flower.

Ask: **How do YOU think we can "Grow From Our Mistakes?"**

Ask and discuss with students what they can learn from the following mistakes?

1. **You made an "F" on the math paper because you didn't read the directions carefully.**

2. **After playing all day, you didn't have time in the evening to finish your homework before bed.**

3. **When you got angry with your brother you yelled and hit him.**

4. **You were throwing the ball in the house and it hit and broke the flower vase.**

5. **You blamed the dog for your mistake in accidentally breaking the flower vase.**

GROWING FROM MISTAKES

Mistakes are the beginning not the end

Fix the mistake

Keep a positive attitude

Improve

Mistakes are gifts of opportunity

Own up to your mistakes

Learn from the mistakes of others

Learn

Change

BRIGHT ATTITUDE

Purpose

To focus on the importance of a positive attitude.

Materials

✓ Copy of the "Your Positive Attitude Brightens Our World" poster on page 57.

✓ Copy of the "light bulb" exercise below. For variety you may choose to enlarge a light bulb, laminate, and allow the student to write their answers on the light bulb with an erasable marker.

Procedure

Ask: **What is a "positive attitude?"**

Refer to the poster and discuss how a positive attitude can brighten the world.

Ask: **Do things go wrong at times?** (Ask for examples.) **Can a positive attitude help when things go wrong? Explain.**

Explain that finding the good in a bad situation is like finding the bright spot or turning on the light bulb to shine in the dark. Ask the student to find the good in the following situations and to write it in the light bulb.

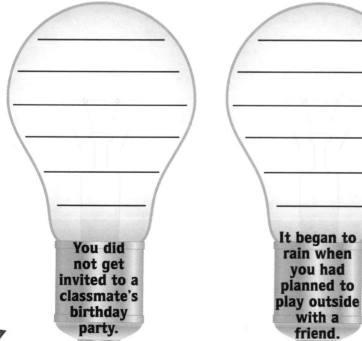

You did not get invited to a classmate's birthday party.

It began to rain when you had planned to play outside with a friend.

Your parents would not let you go see the new movie this weekend.

56

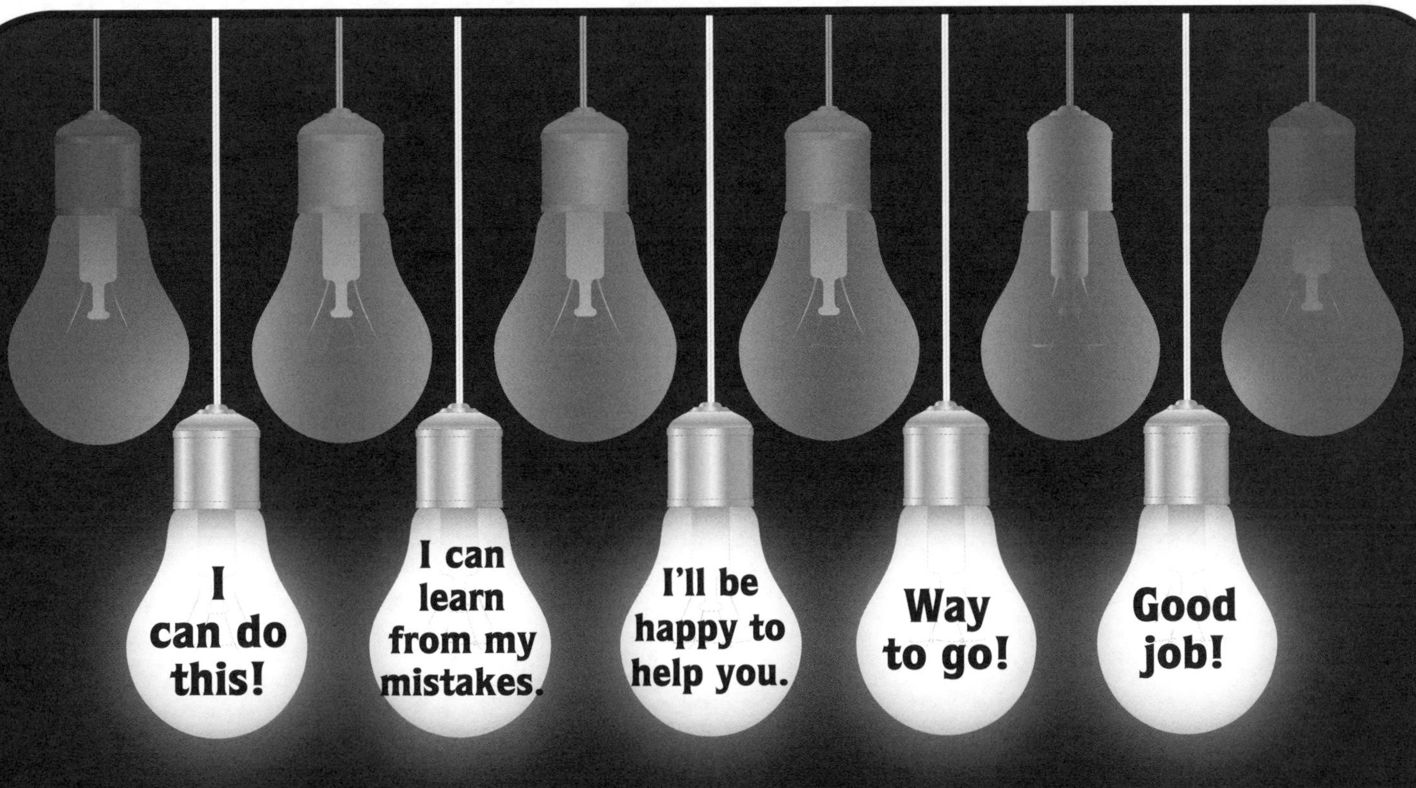

YOUR POSITIVE ATTITUDE BRIGHTENS OUR WORLD

LEARNING THROUGH REFLECTION WRITING

The section provides the opportunity to process (to write as they think and to think as they write), to personalize different learning concepts, and to apply new concepts.

THANKFUL JOURNAL

Purpose

To encourage appreciation for what we have and for what others do for us and to review our responsibility to help and do for others.

Format

The journal can be used with individual students, small groups, or topic introduced through a class lesson or through a school-wide emphasis with teachers using the journals for follow-up.

Materials

✓ Copy the following 2 pages onto 1 sheet – front and back. Next fold, or direct the student(s) to fold, the page into fourths to create a booklet. Fold so that the cover, "I AM THANKFUL FOR…" is the front of the booklet and the days of the week are in order with "MY PLAN…" being the back cover of the folded booklet.

Procedure

Define the word "thankful" by having a student look up the word in the dictionary.

Point out things the children have that they may have taken for granted such as: food, many outfits of clothes to wear, transportation available, toys, a place to learn, etc.

Share that there are children their age in our world that struggle to have enough food to eat, only have one or 2 sets of clothes to wear, have to walk miles to go to the store or school, etc.

Distribute the "I AM THANKFUL" booklets. Ask students to turn to the page "THINGS I AM THANKFUL FOR…" and have them list things in their life they appreciate. Allow time for students to share and allow students to add additional items to their list.

At the end of each day, allow time for the students to write down things people have said or done for them that day that they appreciate. Perhaps you may give examples such as a compliment someone shared or a teacher that helped with a math problem or a friend that talked to them at recess, etc.

Towards the end of the week, ask students to share some of the nice things others have done for them. Discuss the following:

✓ how it felt when someone did or said something nice for them

✓ ways to let the person know what they did or said was appreciated

✓ nice things to say or do for others

At the end of the week summarize the experience. Discuss the importance of giving back to the world and being a positive force. On the back cover of the booklet ask students to complete "MY PLAN FOR HELPING OTHERS…"

Things I am Thankful for...

MONDAY

MY THANKFUL JOURNAL

At the end of each day, stop and think about your day and find at least one thing that you are thankful for. Write or draw about it.

My Plan for Helping Others...

Name: _____

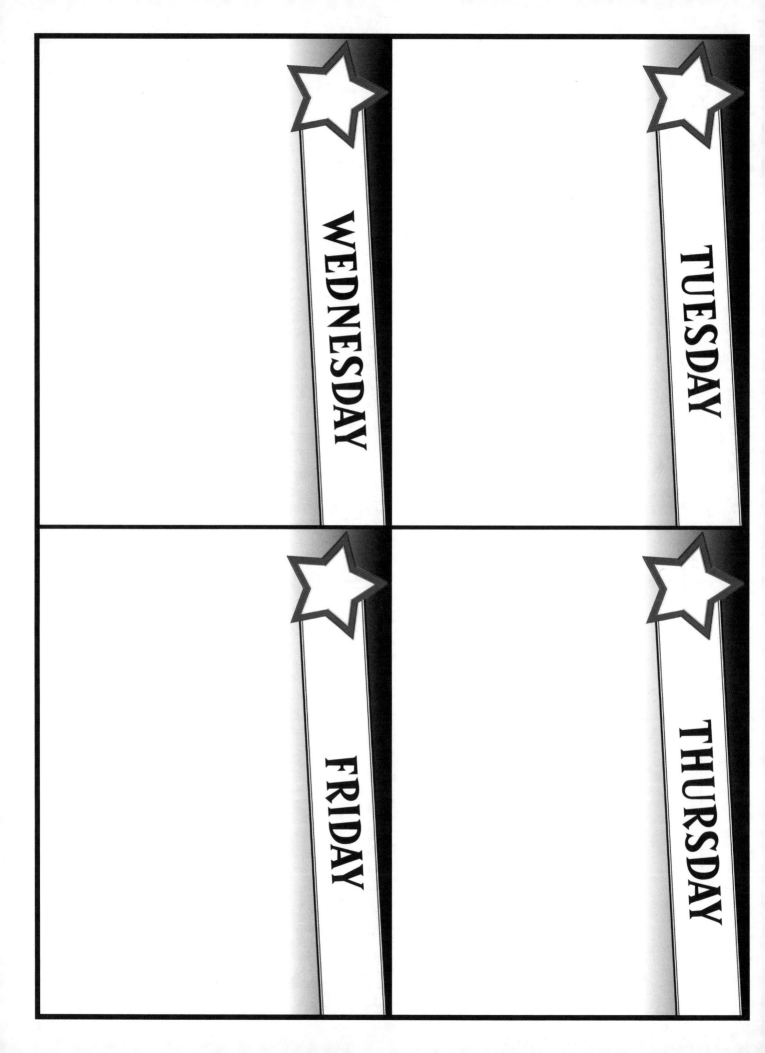

TUESDAY

WEDNESDAY

THURSDAY

FRIDAY

REPRODUCIBLE

REFLECTION ACTIVITY #31

MY DAY IN REVIEW

During my day I: ______________________________

____

____

I was proud of myself when I: ______________________________

____

____

One thing I would change about my day is: (Remember you can't change what someone else said or did but you can change what you would think, say, or do.)

____

____

____

One thing I learned today was: ______________________________

____

____

____

____

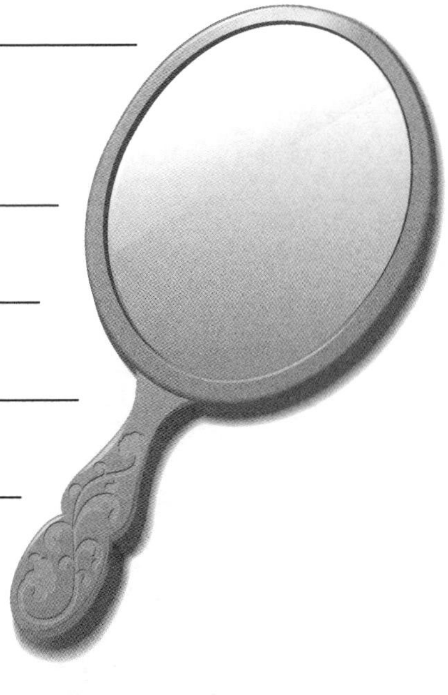

REFLECTION ACTIVITY #32

CHARACTER CONTINUES

Describe how you have seen the character trait of _____
in others today (perhaps in a friend, teacher, parent, or in a story that you read).

_____

_____

_____

How have YOU shown the good character trait of _____
in what you have said or done today?

_____

_____

_____

What is your plan of how you will show the good character trait of _____
tomorrow?

_____

_____

_____

_____

_____

FOOTPRINT PERSPECTIVE

Disagreements come up with our mom or dad, our sister or brother, our teacher, friends, or others. When you have a disagreement with another person, take time to "put yourself in their shoes" to understand what they are thinking and how they are looking at the situation. This may help to understand the situation and work through the problem better.

THE SITUATION:

_____

MY VIEWPOINT

OTHER PERSON'S VIEWPOINT

I think that: _____

_____

So I said or did: _____

_____

The other person may think that: _____

_____

He/She said or did: _____

_____

After "looking" and "thinking" from both viewpoints I now understand _____

_____

REFLECTION ACTIVITY #34

REPRODUCIBLE

GOOD DEED JOURNAL

(Make copies & bind together with a cover to decorate and use as a "Good Deed Journal")

Date: ____________________

Something nice I did for someone today was:

____

I felt ____ after I did something nice.

Happy **Surprised** **Proud** **Pleased** **Nervous**

I think the other person felt ____________________________________.

Date: ____________________

Something nice I did for someone today was:

____

I felt ____ after I did something nice.

Happy **Surprised** **Proud** **Pleased** **Nervous**

I think the other person felt ____________________________________.

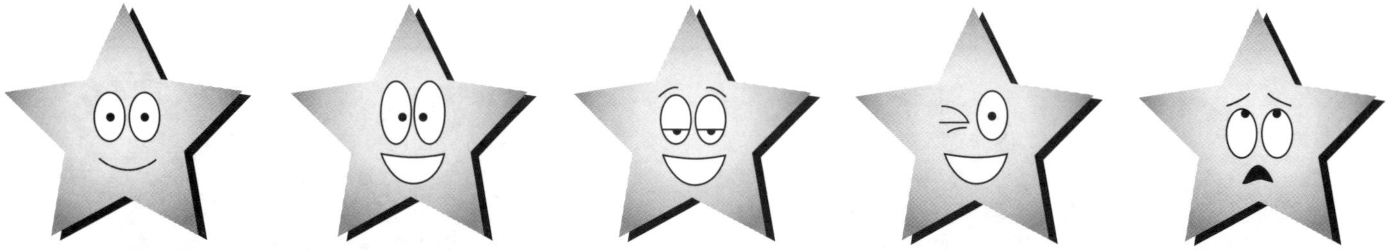

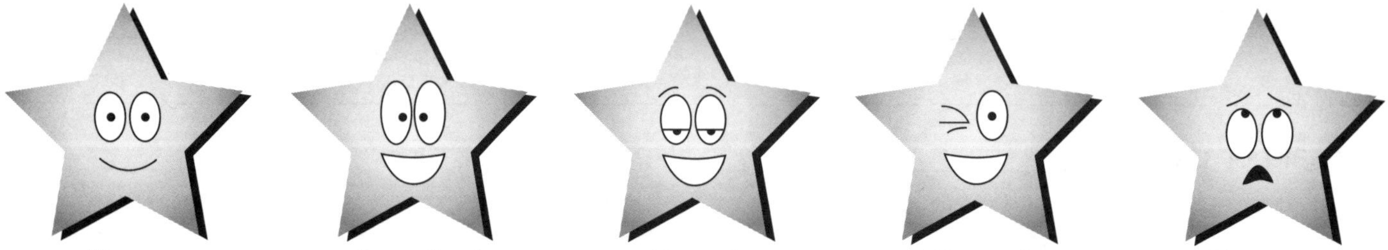

PROBLEM SOLVING POWER

© YouthLight, Inc.

Stop! Take time to think through your problem and a different way to handle it. Use the following to guide you through the process.

My problem is: _____

Brainstorm and list three possible ways you could decide to handle the problem. Then add the "thumbs up" and "thumbs down" of what might happen for each decision.

Choice 1: _____

Choice 2: _____

Choice 3: _____

Review your three possible problem solving choices given above and put a ★ by the choice that you think would work best to solve or manage the problem.

Try it! Did it work?

_____ **Yes, congratulations. Your problem solving power worked!**

_____ **No. Review and try your second choice to solve the problem.**

REFLECTION ACTIVITY #36

BUG OFF!

It really bugged me when:

_____

_____

_____.

Answer the following questions:

Can you change what the other person said or did or what happened?

_____

Is there a different way you can think about what happened or something you can say or do to help the situation? If so, what?

_____

_____

How will you change what you said or did if it happens again?

_____

_____

BUG OFF

Now that you have thought through the situation and made any changes that may be helpful, you now need to LET IT GO. The past is in the past – you don't need to let it bug you anymore. Crumple the sheet up, throw it in the trash, and as you toss it - think "Bug Off Problem."

SHRED THE BAD ATTITUDE

Tear/cut the page above the dotted line and send it through a paper shredder or tear the sheet into small pieces to get rid of that Bad Attitude. Then replace with the New Attitude.

Here's what my BAD attitude looks like:

When other people see my bad attitude, they think: _____

_____

- -

To change my bad attitude, I will: _____

_____

_____

_____

"People are more important than things."

"I can handle this."

"Happiness is a state of mind."

"I can find the good in any situation."

Here's what my NEW attitude looks like:

BRIEF SKITS FOR LEARNING
LIGHTS! CAMERA! ACTION!

This section is great for your kinesthetic learners! Your students will learn not only through participating in the role play but also from seeing the desired skill in action.

PRODUCTION _____

DIRECTOR _____

CAMERA _____

DATE _____ SCENE _____ TAKE _____

RESPECT FOR OTHERS

Purpose

To provide examples, through role play, of 'respect for others' in action.

Format

This brief role play can be used at an assembly program, in a class or with a group of students.

Material

✓ Optional: Puppet

Procedure

Say: **For this next part I need the help of two students in the audience. I need two students that can show respect for each other.**

Direct the students by sharing the following: **Pretend you are in line at the slide – show me how we wait patiently... that's right we show respect for each other and do not push or shove in line.**

Say: **Now let's pretend that we are in class and the teacher is asking a question. Should we blurt out the answer? No. Show me what to do – that's right – raise your hand so we respect others and give others a chance to have a turn answering.**

Direct the students by saying: **Now smile at each other and shake hands and hold that look... Share the following: We need to treat each other in a good way with respect. It is not okay to be mean by what we say or how we look at each other, it is not okay to laugh at people or tease them, it is not okay to call people names, spread rumors, or to leave them out**. Thank the students for their help. Summarize with: **It is important to show respect for each other – on the slide, in the classroom, with each other – everywhere.**

(Optional) Puppet friend can 'pop out' and say: **That sounds like our golden rule would work here, 'Treat others how you want to be treated.' And also, If you don't have something nice to say don't say anything at all.**

RESPECT FOR AUTHORITY

Procedure

Ask: **What is "authority?"** Explain that a person in authority is a grownup who is in charge. It is their job to help make sure that everyone is safe and to help others learn the right things.

Ask: **Who are the grownups in charge at home? In the community? At school?**

Present the following role-plays and discuss:

Purpose

To reinforce respectful behavior to the adults in authority.

CLASSROOM

Scene: In a classroom with students at their desk completing assigned work.

STUDENT: Turn to a classmate and say: **Oh, What are we going to do at recess today? How about if we...**

TEACHER: You need to stop talking and get back to work.

Freeze the role play and ask the following questions (You may choose to have the group give a "thumbs up" or "thumbs down" for their answer):

✓ **Would it be okay for the student to turn back to their work for a minute and then when the teacher is not looking to start talking again?**

✓ **Would it be okay for the student to roll their eyes as they turn back to their work?**

Ask: **What could the student think, say, and do to be respectful to the teacher?**

Unfreeze the scene and allow the student and teacher to complete the role play showing respectful behavior.

CAFETERIA

Share: **This next scene is in the cafeteria with a student in line having a discussion with the adult at the counter about their account. A second student needs another pack of ketchup and rushes up to the adult at the counter... I need a few students to volunteer to set the scene and a student to volunteer to show a respectful way to handle their problem about needing a ketchup packet.**

Have the students create their own role play and process the role play. Point out the importance of showing respect by being patient and not interrupting.

Scene: In the cafeteria a student in line is playing around and making loud noises.

ADULT IN THE CAFETERIA: Goes to the student playing around in line and says: **You need to wait quietly in line.**

Freeze the scene and ask: **Would it be right for the student to ignore that adult just because they are not their classroom teacher? Why not?** Encourage the students to give suggestions of how the student could think, say, and do to be respectful to the adult.

Unfreeze the role play and have the student complete the scene in a respectful way.

Scene: Students on the bus are up out of their seats and being loud.

Say: **Listen to all of the following instructions – Students, you are to pretend you are on that bus, standing and making noises and I will pretend to be the bus driver who will ask you to 'sit quietly in your seat'. At that point, show a respectful response.**

Process the students' respectful responses by complimenting several specific students in what you observed and in asking students what they may have had to think in order to be respectful.

HOMEWORK: ORGANIZATION

Purpose

To prompt discussions of the need and strategies for organization for homework.

Materials

✓ Props for role play: messy notebook, papers

Procedure

Ask for a volunteer to role play the following scene with you about homework. Ask the student to play the "Parent" role while you play the "Child" role.

HOME

PARENT (says in a frustrated manner): **You have wasted enough time to get down to homework. You don't have much time left before bedtime.**

(Child reluctantly opens binder and papers fall out everywhere.)

PARENT: **What's all this? Look at this notebook. What a mess! What is your homework for tonight?**

CHILD: **I can't find my science questions.**

PARENT: **I've just had it with you. Every night it's the same thing – you can't find something. I keep getting these notes from your teacher saying you're not turning things in. What do I have to do, go to school with you to be sure you have everything you need when you need it?**

Process with the following questions:

✓ **How do you think the child is feeling here?**

✓ **How is the parent feeling?**

✓ **Do you think the parent cares about their child getting their homework completed? How do you know?**

✓ **Since you can only be in charge of yourself and not the parent, what do you think you could do to help if you were the child in this situation?**

✓ Brainstorm suggestions for organization.

HOMEWORK: RESPONSIBILITY

Procedure

Ask for a volunteer to role play the following scene with you about homework assignment responsibility. Ask the student to play the "Parent" role while you play the "Child" role.

Purpose

To review the importance of accepting the responsibility to plan for long range assignments and to complete the assignment.

HOME

CHILD: **Dad?**

PARENT: **What is it? You went to bed 20 minutes ago.**

CHILD: **Dad, I just remembered that I have a book report due tomorrow.**

PARENT: **What!?**

CHILD: **My book report is due tomorrow and I haven't finished the book yet.**

PARENT: **How long have you known about this book report?**

CHILD: **I don't know. Our teacher told us about it a couple of weeks ago.**

PARENT: **You've known about this for weeks and this is the first time you've mentioned it to me – the night before the report is due.**

Child begins to whine.

CHILD: **I'm sorry, dad. I just forgot. I thought I'd have plenty of time to get it done. Will you please help me get the book finished and the report done. If it's not done, I'll have to miss recess and I'll get a bad grade and I don't want to get a bad grade. Oh, dad, please help me. I promise this won't happen again.**

Process with the following:

   ✓ **What is the problem here?**

   ✓ **Do you think the dad should help the child get the book finished and the report done? Why or why not?**

   ✓ **What was the responsibility of the student? Was the student responsible?**

   ✓ **Share some helpful strategies or plans that could have helped the child be responsible to get the book report completed.**

Include in the discussion how long range assignments such as book reports or projects may need to be broken into smaller parts, completing a small part each day with the final completion before the due date. Writing these steps on a chart or calendar can help us be responsible and focused to stay on track.

My book report is due tomorrow and I haven't finished the book yet.

STUDENT BAGGAGE
(Teacher Activity)

Materials

✓ Large rocks labeled with a disability or a concern such as: ADD (Attention Deficit Disorder), Autism Spectrum, Family Difficulties, Anxiety Disorder, or Mood Disorder.

✓ Bookbag

✓ Chart paper and marker

Procedure

Take about 10-15 minutes at a teacher meeting for the following role-play.

Say: **Let's think for a moment of what weighs our students down – of the baggage they may carry that makes learning more difficult...** (hold up different rocks with the labels such as ADD (Attention Deficit Disorder), Autism Spectrum, Family Difficulties – may give a brief explanation of the disability.

Purpose

To bring an awareness to teachers of disabilities and concerns that are beneath the surface of each student that may interfere with the student's learning **AND** to brainstorm a list of specific disabilities and concerns that teachers would like additional information about.

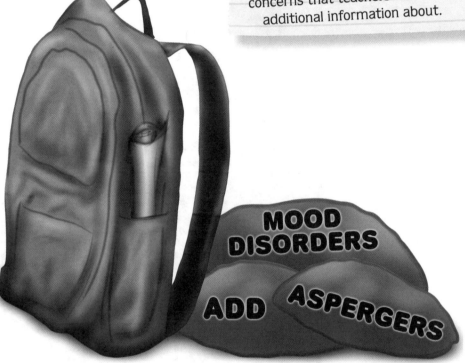

Next, place a rock or two inside the book bag and ask for a volunteer to put on or hold the book bag. Instruct them to walk with the book bag. Ask: **Is that too heavy? Is it doable to walk carrying the bookbag? Do you think it might feel heavy if you had to go everywhere and do everything with the weight of the bookbag? How about if you had to do something more challenging like running, jumping, or swimming with the bookbag?**

Say: **We can relate the weight of the bookbag to the baggage that some children carry – whether it be ADD, family issues, mood disorder, unmotivated, anxiety disorder... You may or may not always "see" the baggage on the outside but when given a different or challenging learning task you may see the frustration of the student surface more easily.**

The first way to help, is for us to have an awareness and knowledge of their disability or difficulty, next is to find ways at school that we can help or accommodate. Sometimes we don't know what baggage they are carrying – sometimes we do know – and sometimes we do know but don't know enough about the problem to help.

Let's brainstorm a list of student disabilities or concerns that you may want to learn more about. Encourage teachers to share as you make a list.

Make your plans to follow up with providing information on the disabilities and concerns that your teachers listed. Some possibilities are:

✓ Provide a "5 Minutes with Guidance" segment at faculty meetings once a month to share information on a specific disability or concern from the list.

✓ Provide written information about different disabilities or concerns throughout the year.

✓ Invite district or community people that are knowledgeable about a specific disability or concern to speak at different faculty meetings or in-services.

KALEIDOSCOPE OF ACTIVITIES

This section is a kaleidoscope or variety of fun activities for learning.

SELF-CONTROL BUTTON

Procedure

When we are working with a class or group of students and a student's interrupting and blurting out is negatively impacting the learning experience for the whole, touch part of your body such as your elbow, nose, etc. and say, **"Use your control button."** The words and the action, typically are enough to help the student process, assess, and make corrections without further discussion.

For some you may need to add their name as you touch your elbow, nose, etc. such as, "Harry, use your control button."

You can also try shortening the phrase to, **"control button."** And then shorten it even more with no words and only the action of touching your elbow, nose, etc. as a reminder while you continue to teach your lesson.

The beauty of this approach is that it takes no explanation. You think we would need to explain what we mean by self-control and how we can imagine ourselves touching a button to change our behavior but students just seem to get it without any explanation.

Variations

Try saying:

- ✓ **"Press your mute button so you can listen"** - when students need to be redirected back to their job of listening rather than talking.

- ✓ **"Press your mute button when you raise your hand"** - when a student is making excited noises with raised hand to be called.

- ✓ **"Turn your volume control down"** - when students are talking too loud.

Purpose

Class or group management strategy to encourage the student to assess and modify poor impulse control behaviors such as interrupting and noises that can be disruptive.

INPUT/OUTPUT – FROM LISTENING TO ACTION

Purpose

To review that listening to someone – truly hearing what they are saying – requires a response or action on our part.

Procedure

Ask: **What do you think is meant by the following sentence?** **"Hearing is an act of the ears but listening involves the ears AND brain, mouth, hands, feet..."**

Review the diagram below and explain how listening goes in the ear when you hear what is being said, then the information goes up to the brain to think about and process what was said and then the information goes to the mouth – to SAY something, or to the hands or body - to Do something. You may choose to use the word "INPUT" for information taken in and the word "OUTPUT" for a response to what we hear.

Allow the students to practice hearing information and responding with the following directions.

✓ Touch your nose.

✓ Raise your hand.

✓ Smile.

✓ Give me a 'thumbs up'.

✓ Talk to the person sitting next to you.

✓ Don't talk.

✓ Say your name out loud.

✓ Sit quietly.

Discuss what it took to be successful to listen to the above directions.

Ask students to give examples of how they have to listen during the day and to describe what they have to do to be successful.

STAND UP AGAINST RELATIONAL AGGRESSION

Purpose

To provide an activity to prompt a discussion of relationally aggressive behaviors.

Procedure

Ask the following STAND UP / SIT DOWN questions:

If you have a cat, stand up... thank you, now sit down.

If you have green eyes, stand up... thank you, now sit down.

If you have ever been teased, stand up... thank you, now sit down.

If you are wearing the color blue, stand up... thank you, now sit down.

If you have ever teased someone, stand up... thank you, now sit down.

If you have ever traveled to an amusement park, stand up...thank you, now sit down.

If you have ever been excluded from something, stand up... thank you, now sit down.

If you have ever excluded someone else, stand up... thank you, now sit down.

If you have a pet dog, stand up... thank you, now sit down.

If you have ever ridden a horse, stand up... thank you, now sit down.

If you have ever repeated a rumor, stand up... thank you, now sit down.

If you have seen the movie ___(fill in with current movie)___, stand up... thank you, now sit down.

If you have ever talked about someone behind their back, stand up... thank you, now sit down.

If you have helped someone, stand up... thank you, now sit down.

Process the activity with any or all of the following questions:

✓ **What do you think about the group's answers? Anyone surprised? Why?**

✓ **Is it fun to be the victim of teasing, exclusion and rumors?**

✓ **For the teasing, exclusion, rumor questions how many of you found that you were both the victim of it and at times have been guilty of doing it to others?**

✓ **Why do you think we are guilty of treating others in a hurtful way when we have experienced how bad it feels to be hurt?**

✓ **When asked if you have ever teased, excluded or spread a rumor about someone, did you hesitate just a little and perhaps were tempted to look around to see if anyone else was going to stand up? Why do you think this may have happened?** Explore the issue of peer pressure and fitting in.

ANOTHER POINT OF VIEW

Purpose

To understand that there are many sides, perspectives, or different ways to look at any situation.

Material

✓ Copy of the illusion picture on page 86.

Procedure

Ask students to look at the optical illusion and share what they see?

Then ask if they can also see...

Ask them to describe what they had to do to be able to see the "other" picture in the same picture.

Ask: **Can there be different ways to look at the same situation? Is there really a right or wrong answer? What does this tell us?**

Say: **When you have a problem with a friend you "see" it from your point of view or thinking... however, can there be a different way to see the same problem? Perhaps they have a different point of view?**

Ask: **How can you understand the way that they are looking at the same problem? Can you listen to them? Ask questions? Try to put yourself in their place.**

RABBIT OR DUCK?

COOPERATION VS. COMPETITION

Purpose

To experience the benefits of cooperation.

Materials

✓ M&M®'s

Procedure

M&M® ARM WRESTLING ACTIVITY*:

- ✓ Ask for 2 volunteers to play a game. Instruct them to sit opposite each other at a table with the elbows of the right hand on the table, then ask them to clasp each others right hand. (You are instructing the volunteers to get in an arm wrestling position without saying the term "arm wrestling").

- ✓ Give the instructions that each time the back of a person's hand touches the table the other person will get an M&M® – caution that the hands need to remain clasped.

- ✓ Allow time for the pair to begin, typically they will arm wrestle, each trying to force the others back of the hand on the table in order to get the M&M®.

- ✓ After the first pair attempts this activity ask for another pair to try. At some point give the hint by asking: **Does anyone know of a way that both players could win more candy?**

- ✓ The secret of success with this activity is for the pair to cooperate and take turns with each person allowing the back of their hands to touch the table. With this approach both are winners with a collection of M&M®'s.

Discuss the importance of cooperating with each other and taking turns with teammates. Use the example of basketball, asking if the team will be successful if one person keeps the ball all the time – review the importance of passing the ball around, assisting each other to line up a basket.

Then discuss the importance of cooperating, taking turns, including everyone, and working together with other types of teams such as a classroom, a project group, at home, at school, etc.

Share Tip: **Rather than focusing on yourself and how you can win, focus on how to work together.**

* original source unknown

BLAST OFF INTO THE FUTURE

Purpose

To creatively introduce a focus on Career Awareness. This activity can be effective with a class or school-wide on morning announcements or assembly.

Material

✓ Recorded sound of a rocket blasting off or a microphone that you can create the noise.

Procedure

Say the following:

Come join me as we blast off into the future....

Whose future? Your future!

We will travel in our rocket time machine into the future.

Close you eyes... (Blast off with the rocket noise)

Wow! We're traveling 15 years into your future.

Open your eyes now...

What kind of job or career will you have in 15 years?

Will you have a job in the health profession? As a doctor, nurse, lab technician?

Or perhaps a job in law enforcement?

Or perhaps in the helping profession as a teacher?

(Give as many examples of jobs as time allows)

There are so many possibilities of jobs out there for you.

We had better return to the present so we can prepare for our future!

Close your eyes and get ready to return (Blast back with the rocket noise)

We're back...open your eyes.

Ask: **How do we start now preparing for our future?**
Include the importance of learning about and being aware of the hundreds of thousands of career possibilities, include the importance of what we learn here at school as the foundation to skills used on the job, include the importance of knowing how to get along with others and handle problems well, and the importance of developing good character for future career success.

FASHION SHOW: MODELING TODAY'S CAREERS

Purpose

To provide a creative visual to review career possibilities.

Materials

✓ Need props/outfits for students to dress up as career models.

✓ Strip of bulletin board paper on the floor to be used as the "runway"

✓ A microphone, if available

Procedure

Prior to the Career Fashion Show, select volunteers to dress up with the career props available. If you are providing the Career Fashion Show schoolwide at an assembly or on a TV morning show, involve the students ahead of time allowing them to choose the career they want to model and encourage them to bring in their own career props and clothes.

Instruct students to walk down the runway with a smile as their name is called, and to 'model' their career outfit.

As the narrator of the fashion show, use your announcer voice and/or microphone to narrate the fashion show such as:

Our first career fashion model is _____. She is modeling a career of a veterinarian. She has her... explain different props – tools of the career – that she is carrying and elaborate on any details of the career that would be age appropriate.

Create your script according to careers chosen to model, props available, and information important to share.

SPOTLIGHT ON CAREERS

Purpose

To provide an opportunity for adults to talk to students about their careers emphasizing how present academics can relate to future jobs and the importance of good character for career success.

Format

Televised morning announcements is an excellent avenue for these brief career talks.

Materials

✓ Copies of the invitation letter to parents, page 91.

✓ Copies of the follow-up letter to parents, page 92.

Procedure

Invite parents to talk about their careers on the televised morning announcements. Send a parent invitation letter (page 91) to let parents know you need their help. You may choose to target one grade level (I typically have done the same grade level each year so students know when they are in that grade they will have the opportunity to invite their parent to talk about their career), or you could put the invitation in a school newsletter, or you can contact specific parents to invite. Encourage parents to bring in items and visuals related to their careers to show.

Ask parents to include in their presentation how academics learned in school are utilized in their career. If your school has emphasized developing good character traits throughout the year, ask the parent to choose one or two character traits and share how that trait relates to their career success. Structure a brief 2-4 minute presentation to include:

✓ Being introduced by their child.

✓ Parent briefly names and tells about their job.

Send the follow-up letter on page 92 to confirm the date and time and provide a guideline for the presentation.

Schedule the "Spotlight on Careers" segment on the morning announcements.

You may choose to take pictures and display for follow up reinforcement of the careers discussed.

"SPOTLIGHT ON CAREERS"
INVITATION LETTER

Dear Parents,

Our school will be focusing on the world of work through career awareness and career exploration through our "Spotlight on Careers." We need your help!

We invite you to come and talk with our students about your career as a guest on our "Spotlight on Careers" segment on our televised morning announcements. We need a brief 2-4 minute presentation about your job.

As part of your presentation on the morning announcements we need you to briefly describe your job, tell specific things our students may be learning in school now that would relate to your job, and share good habits or qualities that you use in your job that make you a better worker. It would also be great if your child could join you on the show to introduce you. We need you to be here by _____ the morning of your presentation – the announcements start at _____ and usually conclude before _____ .

It is important for our students to begin hearing and learning about the many job possibilities for their future. We are scheduling "Spotlight on Careers" on the televised morning show the weeks of _____ _____. If you are able to help, please complete the information and ask your child to return it to his/her teacher or school counselor.

Thank you for considering,

Your School Counselor

- -

Yes, I am willing to talk about my job on the televised morning announcements!

Name: _____ **Career/Job:** _____

Child's Name/Homeroom _____

During the weeks of: _____**Mornings available include:** _____

Daytime phone: _____ **Email:** _____

Thanks for your willingness to help. We will be in touch to confirm and schedule.

"SPOTLIGHT ON CAREERS"
FOLLOW-UP LETTER

Dear

Thank you for your willingness to be a part of our Career Awareness program by agreeing to be on our "Spotlight on Careers" segment on our televised morning announcements to talk about your job.

Your visit is scheduled for _____.

Below is a list of information you may want to include in your presentation. If applicable, you are welcome to include any visuals that correlate to your job or field. **Your child(ren) is/are welcome to be on the televised morning announcements with you to introduce you to the students.** We need you to

be at the school's TV studio located _____.

_____ by _____AM the morning of your presentation.

The televised morning announcements start around _____and usually conclude by _____.

Once again thank you for taking time out of your busy schedule to share with our students as they are learning, growing, and looking to their own futures. If you have any questions or the date scheduled does not work, please feel free to call.

Sincerely,

Your School Counselor

INFORMATION TO CONSIDER INCLUDING IN YOUR PRESENTATION: (2-4 min.)

1. Tell the name of your job and briefly describe what you do.

2. Tell specific things that students may be learning in school now that would relate to your job and help them if they choose your job in the future.

3. Relate how good character traits are important for you to be doing the best at your job. Choose one character trait and share how that character trait is especially important in your job. We have focused on the following character traits this year:

_____.

MARVELOUS MAGIC TRICKS FOR LEARNING

Check out the activities in this section to learn how to perform a few easy tricks and watch the lessons that can be learned.

CRAYON BOX OF FEELINGS*

Purpose

To encourage the acceptance of all feelings and explore healthy ways to manage our unpleasant feelings.

Materials

- ✓ Box of 8 count crayons with a window or opening on the front of the box
- ✓ Scissors
- ✓ Clear tape

Preparation **

Remove the crayons from the box and cut them in half (measure the cut so that when the crayons are placed back in the box they fall below the window or opening). Tape the bottom of the crayons together with clear tape and place back in the box.

Procedure

To perform the trick, turn the box upside down, then pinch or hold tight with your fingers and thumb the bottom half of the box as you turn the box upright. The crayons showing through the window give the appearance of a full box of crayons. Display, what appears to be a full box of crayons, for the student(s) to see as you relate the multi-colored box of crayons to our many feelings, both pleasant and unpleasant. Have the student(s) share their thoughts about the different feelings and connect a color to a feeling. For example: 'yellow' may stand for 'happy;' 'blue' for 'sad;' 'red' for 'mad;' 'orange' for 'excited;' 'green' for 'jealous;' 'purple' for 'afraid;' etc. There is no set color for a feeling so whatever relationship you choose is fine. (If needed, you may go into more detail about feelings by asking for examples of the feelings, role-playing, and sharing the body language of that feeling.)

Ask: **Have you ever been so sad or tired of feeling sad that you wish for all of your feelings to go away?** As you say this, turn the front (window) of the box to the back away from your audience and release the tightness of your hold on the box so that the half crayons drop to the bottom below the window and out of sight. Turn the box back to the audience and it appears that the crayons have disappeared.

Say: **Not only did our blue crayon, our 'sad' feeling, go away but all of our other feelings did also. I don't think we want all of our feelings to go away... I want to enjoy feeling happy and excited. So it looks like we need to get all of our feelings back and instead learn how to manage our unpleasant feelings. I need your help. On the count of 3 say, "Feelings, feelings, come back all."** As the students are calling for the feelings to return, turn the box window away from the audience and upside down. Then pinch the bottom half of the crayon box with fingers and thumb as you turn/flip the box upright with the window facing the audience to display the reappeared crayons.

94

Say: **Now that we have our feelings back we need to learn how to manage our unpleasant feelings. What are some healthy ways that we can manage our sad feelings?** Brainstorm different ways. (You may choose to focus on other feelings with the crayon trick such as mad, afraid, or worried).

Copy, cut out, and display the crayons below. Ask student(s) to tell how the message on the crayon could help manage an unpleasant feeling. Ask the student to complete any other suggestions on the blank crayon.

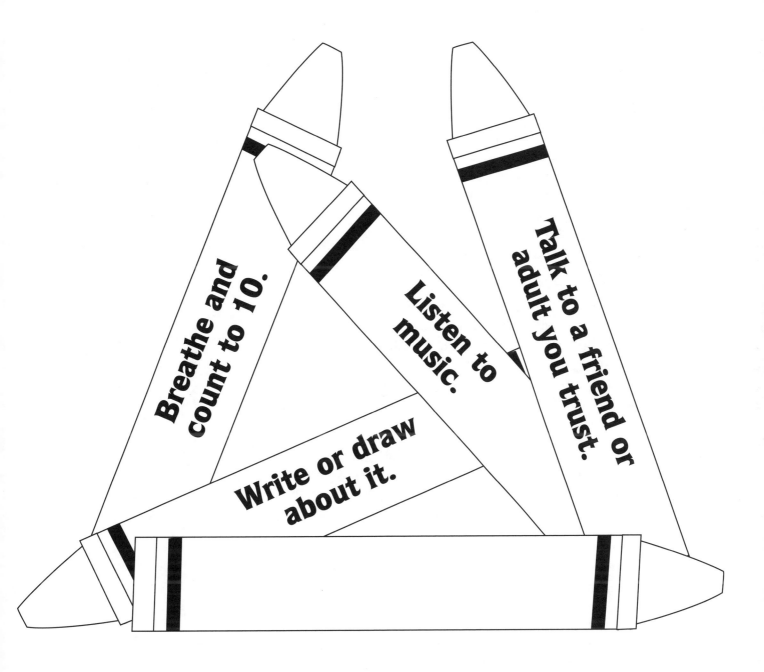

* adapted from R. Bowman, 2004, The Magic Counselor, Chapin, SC: YouthLight, Inc.
** Disappearing Crayons can be purchased through YouthLight, Inc. 1-800-209-9774

BAG POP TRICK*

Purpose

This activity provides a fun way for students to share information and summarize learning.

Material

✓ Paper lunch bag

Preparation

You need to learn and practice the bag pop trick before performing. The intent of the trick is to give the illusion of tossing imaginary rocks/thoughts into the bag – which is great for students to share information and summarize learning. The trick involves three steps:

Step One: Hold the paper lunch bag at the open rim with your middle finger inside the bag, hold your thumb outside the bag but pressed against the middle finger with the bag in between. The other fingers can be outside the bag. The trick is to snap your fingers with the bag in between – this makes the noise as if a rock just fell into the bag.

Step Two: As you are doing the finger snap with the bag, hold the bag relatively steady but perhaps a quick, small downward motion (dipping the bag) as you snap to add to the illusion that the rock just hit the bottom of the bag.

Step Three: The final, yet a very important part of the illusion, is the motion of your eyes and head following the rock being thrown. Your eyes need to be focused wherever the rock is – perhaps your other hand… perhaps being thrown by a student. With your eyes, pretend to follow the rock as it leaves the hand, moves through the air, and lands in the bag (make sure to snap the bag as it lands).

NOW THAT YOU HAVE THE TRICK PERFECTED, THE FOLLOWING ACTIVITIES PROVIDES SOME WAYS TO USE THE TRICK WITH STUDENTS.

* adapted from Robert P. Bowman. 2002. 50 Magic Tricks Using Common Objects. Chapin, SC: Youthlight Inc

© Youthlight, Inc

BAG POP:
STUDENT INTRODUCTION

Purpose

To provide a fun way to have students share their names – great for hearing the names of your new kindergarten students so you can begin getting to know them.

Format

I have found this to be a great activity to use at the end of my beginning of the year introductory lesson with kindergarten students. It captures their attention and they are excited to be involved. Caution: It can be an excitable activity for young students so don't forget to use your good management techniques saying: "Looking for those students sitting quietly to take their turn to toss their rock."

Materials

✓ Paper lunch bag

✓ Ability to perform the BAG POP TRICK – information given on page 96.

Procedure

Hold the open paper lunch bag in front of the student(s), and share that it is full of rocks. Share that you need to empty the rocks on the table, so each student can take a rock, write their name on it and then toss it back into the bag. While you are pretending to empty the rocks, Say: **Oh, did I forget to tell you they are pretend rocks?** Explain to the students that they need to pretend to see the rocks, they need to pretend to catch the rocks as you pretend to throw them, and then they need to pretend to write on their rock a skill learned. Pretend to throw the rocks to the students… and ask them to pretend to write their name on the rock and then hold it quietly in their hand.

Take turns for each student to say their name (reading their rock) and for each student to throw their pretend rock back in the bag. As they throw the rock, perform the trick by following the rock with your eyes giving the illusion, snapping the bag for the sound effect and dipping the bag slightly pretending that the rock is back in the bag. (Do your best to begin learning the names of your new students. Add additional comments about how great they tossed the rock…say their name back…and thank them for the rock.)

When all students have shared their name/rock, don't forget to let the teacher throw a rock if you are doing this as a class lesson, look in the bag and express how excited you are to start getting to know the students and thank them for their help in getting the rocks back in the bag.

BAG POP:
COUNSELOR INTRODUCTION

Purpose

To provide a fun way to have students involved in discussing the role of the school counselor.

Format

Great for a class lesson at the beginning of the year to review with your students the role of the school counselor.

Materials

- ✓ Paper lunch bag labeled as "School Counselor's Bag"

- ✓ Ability to perform the BAG POP TRICK – information given on page 96.

Procedure

Hold up the open paper lunch bag with the labeled side toward the students and have a volunteer read what it says (School Counselor's Bag). Make the comment that perhaps inside this bag we will find something that will help us understand what a counselor does. Look inside the bag, up again at the students with a surprised look and say: **There are rocks in the bag with messages about school counseling on them. Let's look.** At this point, pretend to empty the rocks in the bag onto a nearby desk or table. Pick up a rock and start to read it but then stop abruptly and say: **Oh, did I forget to tell you they are pretend rocks? You have to pretend that you "see" the rock and you will need to listen well to remember the message so you can read the rock back to me and toss it back in the bag.**

Decide the main points of the school counselor's job that you want to communicate to your students such as: Class lessons, small group counseling, individual counseling, and add any specific school-wide programs you may want to highlight. These topics become the titles on each of the rocks you share. As you pick up a rock, pretend to read it as one of the main parts of a school counselor's job. You can explain what it is, ask questions, or give more details after you have pretended to read the title. After you have shared that information about the part of the school counselor's job ask: **Who can tell me what this rock says? What part of the school counselor's job did we just discuss?** Call on a student, pretend to toss them the rock and ask them to read the rock again and then toss it back in your bag.

Continue on until you have covered the basic information for students about what a school counselor does.

For summary, look into the bag again and pretend to read the main titles on the rock, then look up and let the students know that you are excited about a great year together.

BAG POP:
FRIENDSHIP SKILLS

Purpose

To provide a fun way to have students involved in discussing friendship skills.

Format

Great introduction and closing activity for a lesson teaching good friendship skills.

Materials

- ✓ 2 paper lunch bags

- ✓ Ability to perform the BAG POP TRICK – information given on page 96.

- ✓ Optional: lunch bags for each student and crayons, markers, etc. to decorate

Procedure

Ask the students to think of things that people say or do that "HURT" friendships. Hold an open paper lunch bag and call on volunteers to share their thoughts. As they share, ask them to pretend to toss their thought into the bag. As they throw the "thought," perform the Bag Pop Trick by following the "thought" with your eyes giving the illusion, snapping the bag for the sound effect and dipping the bag slightly pretending that the thought is in the bag. After all have shared, look into the bag and summarize the things we may say or do that hurt friendships. Then crumple the bag and toss it in the trash while saying: **So, if these things hurt friendships we need to trash it or get rid of it.**

Say: **Now let's talk about the things that are helpful in a friendship.** Continue with a planned lesson on good friendship skills or have a discussion on friendship behaviors that are helpful.

In summary, hold up another open paper lunch bag and ask volunteers to share things people say and do that are "HELPFUL" in a friendship. As they share, ask them to pretend to toss that thought into the bag. Perform the Bag Pop Trick again as before. After all has been shared, look into the bag and summarize the things we may say or do that are helpful in a friendship. Say, **These are skills we need to keep.**

Optional

You may choose to give each student a bag (especially if you are using with a small group) and allow them to decorate the bag with good friendship skills and take as a reminder.

BAG POP:
END OF THE YEAR SUMMARY LESSON

Purpose

To provide a fun way to summarize the life skills learned from the year's lessons.

Materials

✓ Crayons or markers for students

✓ Paper lunch bag for demonstration and for each student

✓ Ability to perform the BAG POP TRICK – information given on page 96.

Procedure

Hold the open paper lunch bag in front of the student(s), and share that it is full of rocks. Share that you need to empty the rocks on the table, so each student can take a rock, write on it something that they have learned in our lessons together during this year or previous years, and then toss it back into the bag. While you are pretending to empty the rocks. Say: **Oh, did I forget to tell you they are pretend rocks?** Explain to the students that they need to pretend to see the rocks, they need to pretend to catch the rocks as you pretend to throw them, and then they need to pretend to write on their rock a lesson or skill that has been learned through the years. Pretend to throw the rocks to the students…

Ask for volunteers to pretend to read their rock of the lessons learned and to throw the rock back in the bag. As they throw the rock, perform the trick by following the rock with your eyes giving the illusion, snapping the bag for the sound effect and dipping the bag slightly pretending that the rock is back in the bag.

Be a Bucket Filler

Next, explain to the students that you have a bag for each of them that they may first decorate (draw pictures and add words) to help them remember the lessons learned. You may choose to display pictures or words from some of the main lessons to help them with their decorations. Explain that after they have decorated the bag you will teach them the secret of the trick. Hand out bags and crayons/markers and allow time. Remind students that this is a time to decorate their bag with lessons learned and they are not to pick the bag up to try to figure out the trick…patience…

After students have decorated their bag with lessons learned, to add a little fun, you may choose for students to take a "Magicians Oath" before you can tell them the secret to the trick. Ask students to raise their right hand and repeat after you the following:

THE MAGICIAN'S OATH

I (and state your name).
Do hereby pledge.
To never, ever…
Tell the secret of the trick.
Even if they beg and whine
I will not tell the secret.

After the pledge, instruct the student that you will specifically tell them when to pick up their bag but for now they need to listen carefully to the three step instructions. Proceed to first tell them the secret is in a finger snap. You may choose to have students simply practice finger snapping without a bag. Then show them with your bag how to place the finger with the middle finger inside the bag and the thumb outside the bag against that middle finger ready for the snap (you can typically get a clearer sound if the other fingers are placed outside the bag). Next show the students how to gently dip the bag to indicate the rock has landed in the bag. Finally show the important step of following the throw of the rock with the eyes to complete the illusion of the rock throw.

Now instruct the students to stand, open their bag, and practice the trick. As students practice the trick, walk around the room helping, pretending to throw rocks, encouraging and complimenting their ability.

Call an end to the practice, ask students to refold their bag, and encourage the students to keep their bag as a reminder of the lessons learned.

SQUEAKER

Material

✓ Small, plastic, round, flat squeaker that fits in the palm of your hand that when squeezed makes a noise. Can be purchased from magic stores for typically under a dollar.

Purpose

To help with class management for the very young child.

Procedure

When visiting in the younger classrooms – PreSchool and Kindergarten - the squeaker can be used to capture their attention and draw them into participating. It can be used when you have asked a general question to the class such as "Who can tell me what it means to be a good friend?" or "Tell me ways you can be responsible."

Say: **I'm looking for someone who has a squeaky elbow to answer my question.** Call on a volunteer and ask if you can check their elbow first before they share their answer. Take one hand and gently bend the student's arm at the elbow. Place your other hand, which holds the squeaker in your palm, against the student's elbow. As the student's arm bends at the elbow, squeeze the squeaker (that is in the palm of your hand against their elbow) to make the noise. Add your excitement about the student having a squeaky elbow sharing that they must be ready to answer the question. Have the student share their answer and compliment them on being good thinkers and being patient in waiting their turn to be called on.

Next, share that you are looking for a student who is sitting quietly with raised hand that we can check for a squeaky shoulder to give the answer to the next question. Repeat the process.

Vary places to check for squeaks such as knee or ponytail.

Squeaker can just be used at odd times to get their attention and add some fun. It works well if you are wearing clothes with a pocket so when you have finished you can easily put your hands in your pocket and release the squeaker so your hands are free to move on to something else.

STEAMERS: RAINBOW OF FEELINGS

Materials

✓ Multi-Colored Mouth Streamer (package of mouth streamers can be purchased from YouthLight, Inc. 1-800-209-9774)

✓ Picture of a rainbow

✓ Feeling faces

Purpose

To provide a visual analogy relating the many feelings inside of us to a rainbow of colors. This magic trick activity typically works best for the younger student.

The Trick

The multi-colored mouth streamer is a tight ball of colorful tissue paper that when you begin pulling the tissue it provides continuous links of colorful tissue paper. Even though these streamers are advertised as mouth coils and are intended to be pulled from one's mouth, I keep the ball in the palm of my hand and place my hand up to a volunteer's ear and pull the streamer from there.

Procedure

This magic trick is a great visual to add to a lesson about our many feelings inside of us.

Ask: **Have you ever seen a rainbow in the sky? What different colors are in a rainbow?** (Display the picture of a rainbow).

Say: **Think of ourselves like a rainbow. We are not full of different colors but we do have different feelings inside.**

Ask: **What feeling do you think of with each color?** Relate the different colors to various feelings such as: red – mad; orange – frustrated; yellow – happy; green – scared; blue – sad; indigo – proud; violet – shy. You or the student may choose different feelings for different colors, the point is that we are made up of all kinds of feelings both pleasant and unpleasant. Add the feeling faces beside the different colors that you are associating. (If time allows, you can review suggestions on managing each feeling).

Say: **We all have different feelings both pleasant and unpleasant feelings inside of us and it's important that we learn how to manage each feeling. I need a volunteer that I can look in your ear and check out your different feelings inside.** Check with the volunteer to make sure it is okay to look into their ear and pull out their feelings to see.

Perform the trick by having the multi-colored mouth streamer in the palm of one hand. Cup both hands around the volunteer's ear and pretend to look into their ear through your cupped hands. Make comments like... oh, I see your feelings, there they are... begin pulling the streamer from your hand/ their ear to release the stream or links of colorful tissue. Narrate as the tissue is pulled saying: **Oh I see happy, sad, excited, mad, proud...** The intent is to pull the complete streamer from one person's ear but so many want to participate I typically only pull some of the streamer from the first volunteer and then I ask another volunteer and pull the streamer from their ear and then move to another volunteer.

At the end of the streamer you have a very long tissue link as a visual of our many feelings inside of us. Even though the tissue link can not be reused it does make a good class decoration on the wall as a reminder of the lesson. I use this trick at the beginning of the year in kindergarten classes and usually still see the rainbow link on the wall at the end of the year.

104

BUBBLE MAGIC: PREPARE NOW FOR YOUR FUTURE

Material

✓ Wonder Bubbles Magic Trick (can be purchased from YouthLight, Inc. 1-800-209-9774)

Purpose

To emphasize the importance of working hard in school to prepare for your future career.

The Trick

The secret of this trick is in the Wonder Bubbles Bottle that is purchased. The bottle has a false bottom where a small clear ball/bubble is hidden. You first blow bubbles and try to hold onto a bubble but it pops with the touch of your fingers as expected. The trick comes when you give the illusion of holding onto a bubble. This is done by blowing bubbles again however this time when you go to hold onto a bubble you actually palm (hide in the palm of your hand) the hidden clear ball that you let drop from the bottom of the bottle into your hand. You keep the ball hidden in your hand until you reach for the bubble substituting the clear ball for a bubble giving the illusion that you are 'holding onto a bubble'.

Procedure

The bubble trick can be used to reinforce the importance of working hard now in school to help you "hold on to" a good job in the future.

Choose whatever points you would like to emphasize in their lives now that will help them in their future. The three points I have used are:
1. The importance of academics as a basic to future learning
2. The importance of establishing good work habits for future success
3. The importance of knowing how to get along well with others and handle problems

For the trick demonstration share that the bubbles you will blow will stand for the job possibilities for the student when they get out of school. The first set of bubbles you blow represent a student who has not worked hard in school. As you try to hold onto the bubbles (representing holding onto a job) they pop (representing not being able to hold onto a job). For the second student who has worked hard in school, as you blow bubbles and try to hold onto a bubble (the bubble represents a job) you will be able to hold onto the bubble (hold onto the job) which is the trick of the clear ball from the bottom of the bottle that you palmed in your hand.

Say something similar to the following:

For our first student he did not do his best in school, he didn't study, he didn't make the best grades, didn't learn his basic academics, didn't listen in class, didn't do homework, didn't have good work habits, he didn't get along well with others and was not respectful. He did graduate from school somehow and now he is looking for a job, (blow the bubbles and continue saying…) **however he is having trouble holding onto different jobs, he keeps getting fired** (begin popping the different bubbles as you try to hold onto the bubbles, continue saying…) **because he is not doing what he is supposed to or because he is always late or doesn't get along with his co-workers, sometimes he quits because he thinks the job is too hard.**

Next we have a student who worked hard in school. He didn't always make A's on everything but when he made a poor grade he always went back to re-learn the information, he had good work habits with being on time and completing all his homework, and he was very respectful to others and got along well with others. When he graduated from school and was looking for a job (blow a new set of bubbles but this time remove the clear ball from the bottom of the bottle and palm in your hand. Pretend to hold onto a bubble and replace the bubble with the clear ball while holding onto it and say…) **this student was able to hold onto the job of his choice because he had a good academic foundation, had good work habits, and got along well with others. How about you? Are you getting the basics now to help you be successful in your future? To help you hold onto your job? Your future starts NOW – what will you do differently to be prepared.**

106

BUBBLE MAGIC: TRUE FRIENDSHIP QUALITIES

Purpose

To emphasize the importance of developing true friendship behaviors.

Material

✓ Wonder Bubbles Magic Trick (can be purchased from YouthLight, Inc. 1-800-209-9774)

Procedure

Review **The Trick** on page 105 for information on how to perform the Wonder Bubbles Trick.

This trick is a great introduction to a lesson on true friendship qualities, especially powerful with a class or small group of girls that are addressing relational or socially aggressive behaviors.

Give examples describing a girl who uses power, control, and manipulation to have friends. Share that when she is older she is unable to hold onto friends because she did not learn the true qualities that it takes to be a good friend. (Blow the bubbles to stand for friendship connections but pop these bubbles to represent she is unable to hold onto a friend because she never learned the true qualities in friendships.)

Then demonstrate the trick of being able to hold onto the bubbles or hold onto friends as you give examples of a second student who knew the value of being honest, caring, trustworthy, loyal, supportive… in being a true friend who is able to hold onto friendships in her future.

From there the lesson can involve discussions, role-plays, examples, etc. of true friendship qualities and how to develop.

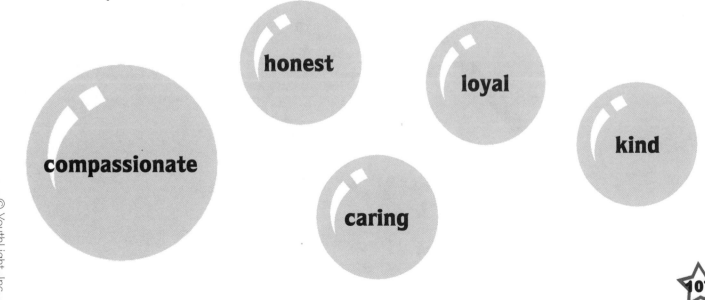

THE MAGIC IS IN YOU

Purpose

To communicate that the true magic is in your abilities and capabilities.

Materials

- ✓ Magic wand
- ✓ Copy of the Magic Wand Message* on page 109

Procedure

Copy the poem and attach to the magic wand. Share that your magic wand has something to say... has a message attached.

Read the message with the student(s) and discuss each part of the poem.

Pose the thought question, How can you use the 'magic in you' to help in everyday life?

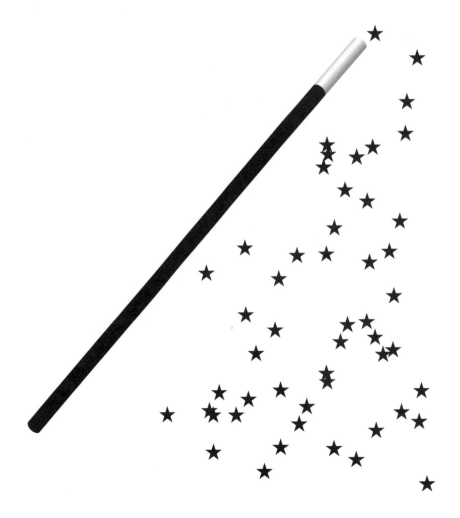

108

MAGIC WAND MESSAGE*

THE REAL MAGIC IS...

IN YOUR HEAD...

when you think
carefully through
difficult situations before
acting on them.

**IT IS
IN YOUR HEART...**

when you are caring and patient
with yourself and others.

**IT IS
IN YOUR ARMS...**

when you reach out to
help someone.

**IT IS
IN YOUR LEGS...**

when you have the courage
to walk up and face your
difficulties honestly.

AND IT IS IN YOUR WHOLE SELF...

when you have the faith that all answers do not lie within you
but you are willing to seek help.

* copied with permission from Bowman, 50 Magic Tricks and the Magic Counselor. Originally written by Bob Bowman.

REFERENCES

Bowman, R., (2002). *50 Magic Tricks Using Common Objects*. Chapin, SC: YouthLight, Inc.

Bowman, R., (2004). *The Magic Counselor*. Chapin, SC: YouthLight, Inc.

Gatewood, B. and Senn, D. (2003). *"Bee" Your Best with Character Ed: A Year Long School Wide Program for Character Development (Grades K-5)*. Chapin, SC: YouthLight, Inc.

Senn, Diane. (2006). *Creative Approaches for Counseling Individual Children*. Chapin, SC: YouthLight, Inc.

Senn, Diane. (2003). *Small Group Counseling For Children*. Chapin, SC: YouthLight, Inc.

Sitsch, G. and Senn, D. (2002). *Puzzle Pieces…Classroom Guidance Connection*. Chapin, SC: YouthLight, Inc.

www.chevoncars.com/learn/food-recipes/candy-names

INDEX BY SUBJECT

INDEX BY SUBJECT